SHADOW BOXING

*The Dynamic
2-5-14 Strategy
to Defeat
the Darkness
Within*

Henry Malone has prepared a cutting-edge handbook for such a time as this. Shadow Boxing *provides a wealth of insights from a mature father of the faith. He not only offers the motivation, but the know-how for turning defeats into victories. This important book is must reading for every Christian.*

Dale Gentry
Founder, Dale Gentry Ministries

Shadow Boxing *is a stimulating and thought-provoking book that offers sound principles. Helpful and easy to read,* Shadow Boxing *equips believers with the necessary tools to turn their lives around. Uncompromisingly honest, Henry Malone's insightful perspective will open your eyes to demonic strongholds, why they exist, and how to rid your life of them. Everyone needs this book!*

Olen Griffing
Founding Pastor, Shady Grove Church, Grand Prairie, Texas

Extremely insightful, yet profoundly simple, Henry Malone provides clues to why so many people continue to suffer unnecessary heartache and defeat. Filled with hope, direction, encouragement, and specific procedures, I wish I had read Shadow Boxing *twenty years ago. I highly recommend this book.*

John Paul Jackson
Founder, Streams Ministries International

Shadow Boxing *reveals not only the principles for living a victorious life, but provides a blueprint for maintaining spiritual health. Henry Malone explains how to deal with root spirits that the enemy has used to keep you from fulfilling your destiny.* Shadow Boxing *will strengthen those who seek to live a dynamic spiritual life and bring freedom to those who are held captive to darkness!*

Chuck Pierce
Executive Director, World Prayer Center

Shadow Boxing *is a timely book for the church. It gives a fresh, biblical, and practical view on how to close the doors to Satan and walk into greater freedom.* Shadow Boxing *is a book that will change your life and give you the keys to seeing your destiny fulfilled.*

James Robison
Founder, LIFE Outreach International

All who want to follow the Lord into deliverance ministry and spiritual warfare can profit from studying this book. Shadow Boxing *has more value than merely setting people free; it is a powerful textbook for equipping warriors greatly needed in the battlefields of ministry. I strongly recommend reading this book.*

John Sandford
Founder, Elijah House, Inc.

Henry Malone's biblical insights on how to prevail against every scheme of the enemy were learned in the white-hot heat of battle. The truths set forth in Shadow Boxing *will free you from patterns of defeats and will loose you into your full potential in Christ. I enthusiastically recommend this book!*

Dr. David Shibley
Founder, Global Advance Ministries

SHADOW BOXING

*The Dynamic 2-5-14 Strategy
to Defeat the Darkness Within*

Dr. Henry Malone

VISION
LIFE
PUBLICATIONS

Lewisville, Texas

First printing, July 1999
Second printing, January 2001
Third printing, January 2003
Fourth printing, August 2004
Fifth printing, February 2006
Sixth printing, February 2008
Seventh printing, January 2011

Request for information should be addressed to:
Vision Life Publications, P.O. Box 292455, Lewisville, TX 75029
Email: info@visionlife.org   Web site: http://www.visionlife.org

ISBN 978-1-888103-16-8
Designed by Ed Tuttle.
Printed in the United States of America.

*This book is lovingly dedicated
to my beloved wife, companion, friend,
co-laborer, and partner of 50 years,
Tina Holloway Malone.
She has offered me
constant love, faithful encouragement,
uncompromising honesty,
consistent support, and diligent labor
which have made this book
become a reality.*

FOREWORD

BY JACK TAYLOR

You are going to love this book, because you can apply these life-changing principles in your everyday life! Dr. Henry Malone knows what it takes to be a winner and he has graciously shared his secrets with the rest of us. *Shadow Boxing* is a simple, balanced, and practical book that contains powerful insights you must follow if you want to live as a winner.

I have known Henry for many years as a friend, pastoral colleague, world missionary, and a scholarly theologian. He is a thinking-man's preacher. Henry's experiences and ministry effectiveness are reflected in his approaches and biblically based principles presented in this book. Using real-life illustrations, Henry brings to life a viable, easily understood, and easily read presentation on a fascinating topic. You cannot walk victoriously without observing these foundational truths.

Shadow Boxing explores the false ideas about what is troubling us and lays an axe to the root of our problems. Henry illustrates his points with interesting case studies and personal anecdotes. His thoughts are well organized and easily remembered. Henry is not merely satisfied that we know why various hardships and difficulties confront us. He seeks to help us break the demonic bondages that enslave us and offers us principles for experiencing greater freedom and abundant living.

If you are a new Christian, this book will jump-start your spiritual growth. If you have been a Christian for several years, this book will make you an even more victorious overcomer.

I heartily recommend *Shadow Boxing*. It will provide you with the necessary tools to help fulfill your God-given destiny. It also offers a blueprint for leaders who seek to raise up ministry teams to bring inner healing and deliverance to those in the Body of Christ. May God's anointing rest upon this book's publication, distribution, and usage in the global advancement of the glorious Kingdom of God.

Jack Taylor
Founder, Dimensions Ministries, Melbourne, Florida

CONTENTS

ACKNOWLEDGMENTS

I want to express my appreciation to all those who, over the few past years, have encouraged, helped, supported, and believed in me. First and foremost, I would like to thank my wife, Tina, and my children Bart, Kimberly, and Shaun Malone as well as my grandsons Daniel and Austin and my granddaughter Hannah, who are not only the most important ministry in my life but also my greatest joy.

I want to thank Gayle Watkins, who transcribed many hours of audiotapes; Dian Green, the first ministry intern who insisted that I put this material into a book; Marigene Lindsey and Mike Mugavero who were not only ministry interns but great friends who believed in me and in this endeavor. I also want to acknowledge all the other ministry interns who ministered with me over the last several years; we have grown wiser and learned more together.

I want to thank Dale Gentry, a faithful friend who has profoundly influenced my life for more than fifteen years. I am also deeply appreciative of my pastor, Olen Griffing, whose single-hearted love for Jesus and a lifestyle of genuine humility has significantly impacted my life.

I want to acknowledge the special friends and partners who contributed financially to support the publication of this project. Thank you for your vision and generosity in expanding the Kingdom of God.

And finally, special thanks goes to Margie Knight, John and Brenda Ward, and Carolyn Blunk who spent many hours immersed in editing and proofreading this manuscript because they believed in the Truth which sets us free.

INTRODUCTION

In the spring of 1973, I was a young pastor seeking God and asking Him to pour out His Spirit upon my congregation. Although sincerely hungry for the things of God, I was not prepared for the unique way He would answer my prayer. I want to share with you the pilgrimage on which God took me. What He did for me, He can do for you.

As a three-day revival meeting turned into three weeks of nightly meetings, God visited us with supernatural manifestations of His power. What I discovered was much different than any human mentoring or natural educational process I had ever experienced. The Holy Spirit arrived bestowing upon us a genuine taste of His power and presence. In the midst of that visitation, my life was radically and instantly changed. I discovered that when a person experiences a divine encounter with God's Spirit, a process of transformation begins.

Although I had known Jesus Christ since the age of eleven, the landscape of my life was cluttered with debris that I was constantly hiding. Strong negative emotions like anger, fear, jealousy, and lust grew profusely in the soil of inferiority and inadequacy. I planted flowers around these weeds to hide their ugly appearances. When the flowers were not tall enough to hide the weeds, I planted rose bushes, shrubs, and hedges to protect myself so others would not discover who I really was on the inside. After all, I was a pastor!

By sheer grit and determination, I tried to keep these fleshly attitudes inside and somewhat under control. Forced to keep a cork in my bottle, I was weary of wrestling with the contents on the inside. These internal struggles began to unravel the spiritual fabric of my life. I often cried out to God, "Lord, there must be more than what I am experiencing! Is there a way to get rid of the vile filth inside me once and for all? Is there a way to silence the screams and demands of the dark shadows that plague me?" My attempts to ignore or hide from these demanding thoughts only led to further defeat in my life.

Then, God answered my prayer. In one dramatic encounter with the God of power, the satanic strongholds in my life were broken, lies were exposed, and the enemy's chains around my life were cut. The prison in which I had lived since birth opened, and I walked into more freedom than I had ever experienced. Literally, I became a new man. My soul, which had shriveled to a worm-like existence, became a soaring butterfly. Instantly my family recognized something was different. My associates realized my life had changed. Outwardly I was the same, but the internal battle had ceased. Although the war was not over, I had discovered a significant key to continually walking in righteousness. I was no longer forced into Satan's hammerlock over my mind and actions. I had discovered how to be freed from the oppressive, dark forces around me.

In 1973, talking about evil spirits, demonic strongholds, and the kingdom of darkness was taboo. The two groups who talked about demons were either the insane or those who were considered extremist, religious fanatics. I knew that I belonged in neither of those camps. While these topics are talked about openly and easily today, back then anyone who talked about demonic strongholds was perceived as being a strange "kook," a religious "nut," or a weirdo. As a result of this widespread attitude, few people were willing to discuss spiritual warfare and its implications for Christians.

My road to discovery and freedom was lonely at first. God seemed to thrust me into the personal ministry arena, hand me a red cape, and say, "Here come the bulls. Learn how to deal with them." Well, deal with them I did! Since that time, I have been on a steep learning curve. Over the years, God has taught me by revealing truths in His Word and by His Spirit. He has instructed me through learning by trial and error and by what I could glean from others. I read every book I could find on the subject and asked people to share their life stories with me. As a traveler on the journey, I continue to pray for insight and revelation that will cause me to walk in greater Christlikeness with each passing year.

The book you are about to read is a capsule of the principles I have learned. I call it the 2-5-14 strategy. Basically, there are two ways Satan has access to our lives—by intrusion or by operating through open doors that give him legal access to torment and harass us. There are at least five doors that give Satan legal access to our lives—ancestral curses, disobedience, unforgiveness, emotional trauma, and inner vows and judgments. These doors may be opened by our own actions or as a result of the residual effects from the sins of our ancestors. In addition, there are at least fourteen evil spirits that the Bible names specifically as spirits—infirmity, fear, divination, whoredoms, bondage, haughtiness, perverseness, antichrist, deaf and dumbness, heaviness, lying, jealousy, stupor, and error. (In later chapters, I will give you the scriptural references for each of these spirits as we study them.) These fourteen spirits are the root system by which Satan works his schemes in our lives.

By studying biblical passages and personal case studies, we will examine how these powerful principles operate. We will also explore how to gain victory over the enemy in every area of our life. I pray that these insights will transform and empower you to walk in the freedom that Jesus provides for you. He came to give us life and to free us from the torment of the enemy. None of us are as free as Jesus died for us to be. Even if we know Jesus as our Savior, most of us still have demonic strongholds and curses operating in our life that need to be broken. Only by the blood of Jesus and the power of the Cross can strongholds be dismantled, curses broken, and roots cut. The blood required only Jesus' death but the Cross requires our death with Him.

I have been crucified with Christ; it is no longer I who live, but Christ lives in me; and the life which I now live in the flesh I live by faith in the Son of God, who loved me and gave Himself for me—Galatians 2:20.

We need to receive the ministry of Jesus which is outlined in Luke 4:18, "The Spirit of the Lord is upon Me, because He has anointed Me to preach the gospel to the poor; He has sent Me to heal the broken-hearted, to proclaim liberty to the captives and recovery of sight to the blind, to set at liberty those who are oppressed." As we allow the Lord to set us free from the chains that bind us, we can experience all of the benefits described in this passage of Scripture.

I rejoice that Jesus has set me free and continues to set me free each day, by the power of His blood and by picking up my cross and following Him. Each of you can find freedom, if you will receive by faith all that Jesus has provided for you.

PART 1

REALITY OF THE SPIRIT REALM

CHAPTER 1

ON THE ROPES OR IN THE RING?

A boxer stands in the center of the ring, decked out in all the right gear—satin boxers, padded leather gloves, and a helmet. He has the confident look of a winner. Yet each time he lunges for his opponent, trying to connect a right hook into his jaw, his fist boxes the air. There is no connection. His opponent may seem real, but the boxer has been wearing himself out in the ring for nothing. Thinking he was hitting the target, the fighter has merely been boxing at shadows. All his expensive boxing gear, fancy footwork, and carefully planned punches will get him nowhere.

Boxing at shadows is a futile exercise. It does not accomplish anything except to tire you out. It leaves you sweating against the ropes, sucking air, and feeling frustrated, defeated, and ashamed.

This book is for the tired, the defeated, the frustrated, and the ashamed. It is for the hurt and broken, those walking in powerlessness and fear. It is for all who have found truth but are failing miserably at living it. It is for those walking in bondage and limitations imposed by dark forces over which they seem to have no control. It is for those who secretly wonder why their lives do not portray the overcoming reality God has purposed. It is for those to whom it seems a strong unseen hand holds them to a course they feel incapable of changing. And, most importantly, this book is for Christians who find themselves spending more time "on the ropes" and in the sidelines than in the ring of life.

Perhaps you are puzzled by utterly devastating defeat—many are, even though they're Christians! You have accepted Jesus Christ into your life, but you all-too-willingly succumb to destructive circumstances that come your way. Even knowing that God has provided a way for you to walk in His Light, you continue to wear yourself out, boxing at the shadows of temptation and destruction. You know more truth than you are living. You are not alone. In fact, you may be among the majority in the church today. Frustration and defeat have dimmed our spiritual light in an increasingly dark and wicked world.

THREE REASONS FOR DEFEAT

I see three prevailing reasons for the cycle of frustration and defeat that marks the lives of Christians today.

First: Many believers deny the existence of the spiritual realm, and/or have a lack of knowledge about how the spiritual realm operates. The spiritual realm does exist. In fact, there's an explosion of fascination in our country today. Many non-Christians recognize the existence of a spiritual realm. They are fascinated by occult, psychic, and mystical powers. Many allow themselves to be allured by the darkness. Likewise, many national leaders seek guidance from astrology, Ouija boards, seances, and psychics rather than from the

Scriptures, listening to the voice of God, or from the Lord's prophets.

This alarming trend has created a weapon that is far more deadly than one that a mortal enemy could have devised. It has unleashed a demonic onslaught of unprecedented proportions.

Tragically, the church has been asleep. She has not arisen to engage in the powerful God-given undertaking of proclaiming and demonstrating the works of Jesus. Not only is the church failing to display God's supernatural works, but she is delinquent in training believers about the spirit realm. Believers are not being taught biblical keys to successful spiritual warfare! Whether certain churches agree, God is supernatural. He transcends the laws of the natural realm. Ignoring the realm of the supernatural will not make it disappear. In fact, consider how a lack of knowledge about the spiritual realm played a role in the following story.

SUE'S STORY

Having just become a Christian, Sue was dangerously suicidal. She had left her husband and children and told me tearfully that I was her last hope. As I listened to her story, it became apparent that Sue was controlled by the spirits of fear and divination. She was distraught and could hardly function mentally. Her lifetime involvement in witchcraft included, among other things, astral travel and talking with "spirit guides." These spirit guides even offered her business advice. Fear had emotionally paralyzed Sue and caused her to move in and out of reality. Unable to sleep for days, Sue lived with hallucinations and saw demonic spirits and faces.

As we talked, I discovered that various forms of divination were commonplace in Sue's family. Family members frequently played with the Ouija board and were regularly involved with seances. When Sue

11

was just a child, her mother took her to fortune-tellers; this was repeated many times as she grew older. Sue thought that dabbling in divination or witchcraft was normal.

A spirit of immorality had a strong presence in her family as well. As a young girl, Sue was molested by people who frequented her home for witchcraft purposes. This created great stirrings of lust in her life. During her teenage years, she became sexually promiscuous with every boy she dated and she began to experiment heavily with drugs and alcohol. After graduating from college, she eventually married a young man with whom she had a long-term sexual relationship. Sadly, Sue was plagued with deeply rooted feelings of inferiority, low self-esteem, and a poor self-worth.

As I ministered to Sue, God moved mightily to set her free from the dark spirits of divination and fear, as well as numerous other spirits. Deep wounds of rejection were healed. Sue's life was changed that day. A few months later, I discovered that she had reconciled with her husband and children. She no longer suffered from fear, and her suicidal thoughts were gone. Demons no longer talked to her anymore. She was regularly attending church with her husband and children. Together, they were growing in the knowledge of the Lord Jesus Christ and God's spiritual realm!

Denying or minimizing the existence of the spiritual realm and walking in ignorance concerning spiritual warfare will force you to live "on the ropes" spiritually. You will find yourself hemmed in, cut off, defeated, shut down, and assigned to a menial, miserable existence. You may feel locked into an unfulfilling marriage at best and "hell on earth" at worst. You may be involved in destructive or sinful relationships, that keep you repeatedly stumbling and falling in your spiritual life. Let's face it. When we live in denial, we are not going to experience the powerful and abundant life that Jesus came to give us.

Second: You may be losing the "rounds" in your life, because you have bought into an age-old lie of the enemy. You may believe that you cannot become more than you are right now. You may unknowingly have accepted a victim mentality and thereby reject embracing an overcoming mentality. If this is the case, you are walking in deception, without a clue as to who you really are!

Would it surprise you to know that through Jesus Christ you have the power to live a victorious and overcoming life? Did you realize and apprehend that when you accepted Christ and were filled with the Holy Spirit, that you obtained the ability to become an aggressive overcomer? Were you aware that, through Christ, you could actually win? To do so, however, requires that you take hold of all that the Cross has provided—and experience this liberating truth by faith. You cannot remain passive.

Victory does not come automatically. To be an overcomer, you must rise above and outmaneuver, conquer and aggressively resist enemy forces. Even in that effort, God has given you power, but you must apprehend it undauntedly as you persevere in faith! Step forward. Take your place and tenaciously enforce your sure and certain victory. Otherwise you will never experience the triumph God has given you through Christ.

POSSESSING THE LAND

God's dealings with Israel are an example for us today. To see the principle of a victorious, overcoming life defined more clearly, let's look at a passage in Scripture.

God said to Israel: "Behold, the Lord thy God hath set the land before thee: go up and possess it, as the Lord God of thy fathers hath said unto thee; fear not neither be discouraged" (Deuteronomy 1:21).

God told Israel to go and possess the land of Canaan. Notice that even though God had already given them the land, possessing the land was still up to Israel.

> *Strategy for Today:* **God has given you authority over the shadows, but to overcome, you must use that authority! To overcome, you must possess the land! As with Israel, there are areas in your life that you still need to possess! The "land" that a Christian must learn to possess is located in three areas of life: the body, soul, and spirit.**

BODY, SOUL, AND SPIRIT

Each of us has a body, an "earth suit" housing both soul and spirit. The soul is composed of three parts—the mind, the will, and the emotions. The soul enables us to think, feel, and make decisions.

The spirit has a three-fold purpose—communion, intuition, and conscience. When we worship, we do so through communion, which is the spirit's ability to meet and experience another—specifically, God. Through the spirit's intuition, we know or learn without the conscious use of reasoning. The gifts of the Holy Spirit flow out of our intuition. Our conscience is a sense of moral rightness. It is the part of our spirit upon which God has written His moral law, enabling us to know right from wrong.

Created as a triune being in the image of God, mankind is subject to the enemy's attack in all three of these areas. Satan attacks our body with disease. He infiltrates our mind with lies and deception; he laces our will with rebellion; our delicate emotions are fragmented and hardened by pride, fear, jealousy, and other negative attitudes. With gleeful delight, Satan raises up strongholds against our knowledge of

God so that we are incapable of communing with or worshipping our loving heavenly Father God. His image is distorted by the enemy's shadows.

The quest to live the victorious life lies in learning how to possess all that God has already given. We need to become dissatisfied with living a subnormal life that we call normal. We need to stop letting the dark shadows block the pure light and joy of the Spirit of God. He has given us His light! Take it, walk in it, and use it to drive out the shadows of Satan's demonic spirits and strongholds. They are trespassing and have no legal right to torment us any longer.

ISRAEL'S WANDERING

When the children of Israel began to journey from Egypt to Israel—the promised land—it was not God's design for them to wander in the wilderness for forty years. But because of their unbelief and hardness of heart, they were not allowed to go in and take possession of their land! Since they did not trust in the Lord's provisions, they walked in circles, going no place in particular—and then they died in the wilderness! (See Numbers 14:22–29; Ezekiel 20:13.)

> *Strategy for Today:* **Determine to possess your land and fight the darkness, or you will spend the rest of your life walking in circles!**

Israel refused their new identity in Him. The battle was the Lord's, but they did not trust Him to fight it. They did not believe that the same God who had given them the land would empower them to drive out the entrenched inhabitants of the land. Actually, the people living in Canaan had heard of Israel's great God and were "quaking in their boots." Israel simply needed to go in and take the land.

After Israel's forty years of wandering, a new generation arose that was fearless. They believed God and had a mindset of conquering. By miraculously parting the swollen waters of the Jordan River, God led this new generation through on dry ground. In Canaan, they faced a land with thirty-one kings and three kingdoms.

> *Strategy for Today:* When we accept Christ we, too, must face kings and kingdoms that have become entrenched in our minds and souls. In Jesus, we have access to purity and godliness and are given every spiritual blessing. But we carry an array of dark kings that once ruled our lives. These demonic rulers want to keep us from possessing the promises of what has been given to us legally. In essence, they want to hinder us from walking in the Light.

Often, these dark rulers seem normal to us because of our everyday struggles, familiar patterns of thinking, and routine behaviors that have been handed down in our families for generations! The "iniquities of the fathers" have been passed to us as their children. Often, we do not even recognize these behaviors and thoughts for what they really are! Anger, inferiority, fear, anxiety, jealousy, lust, infirmities, pride, haughtiness, control, and arrogance have been inherited from those who walked before us, beginning with Adam!

This concept is evidenced earlier in Sue's story. Sue received a spiritual inheritance when she accepted Jesus as her Savior, but she had to take back the land from the demonic spirits who had been given access to dwell there as a result of generational sin as well as Sue's own sin. Through repentance and prayers of deliverance, Sue reclaimed her land and closed the doors to demonic access in her life. Once she did these things, Sue was able to live more fully in the inheritance that was given to her by Jesus Christ.

None of us are as free as Jesus intended for us to be. We may be as free as we know how to be at this hour. As we gain new freedom, we will then be able to look back and see how deeply in bondage we were all along. When we are born again by the blood of Jesus, we are given a spiritual inheritance. We must reclaim our body, soul, and spirit from the dark forces that have controlled us. We must drive out the dark shadows in order to walk in the pure light that Jesus provided for us by His birth, death, and resurrection.

On the Cross, Jesus broke the power of the kingdom of darkness. "Having spoiled principalities and powers, He made a public show of them openly, triumphing over them in it" (Colossians 2:15). Through the power of the blood and the Cross, Jesus broke Satan's power which enables us to walk in freedom. Our position is the same today as it was for the children of Israel. We must possess the land of spiritual freedom or remain lost in the wilderness of defeat.

Third: Willingness to compromise with the enemy is one of the major causes of failure in the life of the believer.

If you decide to live with the enemy, you will eventually watch the enemy rise up and return you to bondage. If you commit yourself to rising up and taking control of your body, mind, and spirit, God will give you total victory over the enemy. No matter what price you may have to pay, the outcome will be worth it.

When you tolerate the dark places inside yourself and settle down to live with them, the enemy will become stronger while your spirit grows weaker. At every clash or contest in which you desire but do not accomplish it, you will lose the round. As long as you are willing to compromise and live with the enemy, that is right where you will remain. No contest. No clash. No progress. No victory.

AN ENEMY CALLED CONTENTMENT

If the enemy cannot induce you to compromise, he will cause you to become content with what you already have rather than press in to fight and to possess all that is rightfully yours. Don't settle for second-best! Accept the challenge today and get off the ropes and into the ring so that you can possess all God wants for you.

Possess the land of your will. Do not remain passive in your actions and activities. Possess the land of your emotions by refusing to be hurt or experience rejection. Possess the land of your flesh and live righteously. Do not be dominated by evil. Draw a line in the sand and say to the kingdom of darkness, "No more!"

God will not show up until you challenge the enemy. Once you challenge the kingdom of darkness, God will come on the scene with power. When you face the enemy in faith, the battle is the Lord's. Rise up, get off the ropes, and take your inheritance—all of it. Then you will walk in the victory that is rightfully yours.

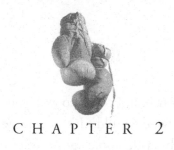

STILL SHADOWBOXING YOUR DARK SIDE?

We cannot ignore the fact that Jesus spent a third of His ministry casting out demons—dark shadows. As His followers, we are called to do the same. We need to remember that we do not have to be overcome, beaten down, run over, and shot through by the enemy. We are called to advance the Kingdom of God. Thereby, we have been given authority over the kingdom of darkness (Matthew 28:18-20).

Believe it or not, it is possible for a believer to be demonized. However, it does not mean that the person is possessed. Demonic possession is a term meaning demonic ownership. A Christian who belongs to God cannot be owned by a demon. But the demonic realm does own the souls of those who are lost.

The real issue is control. If a demon can control your thoughts and actions, it does not need to own you! For example, if you allowed me to borrow your car anytime I wanted to borrow it, I wouldn't need to own a car. I could do with your car the same thing that you as the owner could. It's the same in the life of a person controlled by a demonic spirit. Why own what you can borrow?

A Minister's Story

A young minister who had been in the ministry for ten years telephoned and asked for my help. He came to my office and shared his story. Having been raised on a ranch, he had lived a wholesome life. His parents were devoted Christians, although they were unaware of the workings of demonic forces.

Beginning at the age of ten, this minister had been molested by an uncle. While he loved this uncle, he felt incredible shame. Yet, he did not know how to get out of the harmful relationship. He felt trapped. His uncle introduced him to pornography and supplied him with all kinds of pornographic materials—magazines and explicit sex videos of increasing degradation. By the start of ninth grade, the young boy became sexually involved with girls. He fell in and out of promiscuous relationships. When he was a senior in high school, his first true love—the girl he thought he was going to live with for the rest of his life—became pregnant. She had an abortion, which broke his heart. Six months later, after she ended their relationship, the young man married someone else. He loved his wife, but because of the soul tie with his one true love, he never could get over her.

After graduating from college and seminary, he became a minister. Hooked on pornography since childhood, he hid his sinful habits. Over the years, he was unfaithful to his wife and had many affairs. He snuck out to peep-shows and massage parlors and had sex with prostitutes.

No one knew anything about his double life or his sexual addiction.

Yet the guilt and condemnation he felt caused a deep depression. He lost weight, his health spiraled downhill, and he even contemplated suicide. Desperate for help, he was too ashamed to confess to fellow ministers that he was a sex addict.

A friend told him about my ministry. As we began to seek the Lord for help, we called up the deep pain from within his spirit—the rejection from a father who had little time to spend with him, the trauma of repeated molestation from his uncle, and the incestuous relationships that followed with various cousins. He repented of his sins and forgave those who had hurt him. We rebuked the spirits off his life and broke the curses attached to these dark spirits. Today, he is free from the sin, guilt, and shame of the past. He is now a loving husband and a capable minister of the gospel, free from the tormenting shadows within.

MISSING THE POINT

One of the most effective ways to take the heat off one person is to turn the heat up on someone else. This is exactly what has happened when Christians began to ask one another, "Can a Christian have a demon?" We—the church—have missed the whole point. We have focused on our theology about Satan and his demons and have not learned how to stand against these evil ones.

There are many theological views concerning the demonic realm operating in the lives of believers. Many believe that because they are saved and filled with the Holy Spirit, a demon cannot live inside, alongside the Holy Spirit. Others do not believe in demons at all, and therefore, do not believe they can be affected by them! The truth about whether or not a believer can have a demon is found in God's Word.

Jesus made the following statement to the Canaanite woman whose daughter was severely demon-possessed:

> *Then Jesus went thence, and departed into the coasts of Tyre and Sidon. And behold, a woman of Canaan came out of the same coasts, and cried unto him, saying, Have mercy on me, O Lord, thou son of David, my daughter is grievously vexed with a devil. But he answered her not a word. And his disciples came and besought him, saying, Send her away, for she crieth after us. But he answered and said, I am not sent but unto the lost sheep of the house of Israel. Then she came and worshipped him, saying, Lord, help me. But he answered and said, It is not meet to take the children's bread, and to cast it to dogs. And she said, Truth, Lord; yet the dogs eat of the crumbs which fall from their masters' table. Then Jesus answered and said unto her, O woman, great is thy faith: Be unto thee even as thou wilt. And her daughter was made whole from that very hour—Matthew 15: 21–28.*

The Canaanite woman came to Jesus asking Him to cast the demon out of her young daughter. Jesus called the woman a dog, which was a cultural term for non-Jews (Gentiles or unbelievers). Jesus told her that the bread (deliverance) belongs to the children (believers). He explained that it was not for the dogs. The woman humbly replied, "Yes, Lord. But even the dogs get to eat the crumbs which fall from the master's table."

Strategy for Today: Jesus stated clearly that deliverance is primarily for the believer! However, Jesus also gave the "children's bread" to the Gentiles. Sometimes God gives a miracle of deliverance to an unbeliever as an avenue for salvation, for an unbeliever's mind may be so ensnared that some deliverance is necessary before he or she can exercise their will to choose Jesus Christ. (See 2 Corinthians 4:3–4.)

In the New Testament, we see believers often being controlled or demonized. In the Book of Mark, a man in the Jewish synagogue was demonized. The demon spirit cried out when Jesus addressed it and told it to leave.

> *And there was in their synagogue a man with an unclean spirit; and he cried out, saying, Let us alone. What have we to do with thee, Jesus of Nazareth? Art thou come to destroy us? I know thee who thou art, the Holy One of God. And Jesus rebuked him saying, Hold thy peace, and come out of him. And when the unclean spirit had tormented him and cried with a loud voice, he came out of him. And they were all amazed, insomuch that they questioned among themselves, saying, What thing is this? What new doctrine is this? For with authority commandeth He even the unclean spirits, and they obey Him—Mark 1:23–27.*

This man had to have been a believer in Jehovah, or he would not have been allowed in the synagogue.

DEMONIC ACTIVITY

It is possible for a believer to have a demon. The manifestation of demonic spirits occurs in specific ways. Just as there are certain characteristics and principles at work in the physical world, such as the laws of physics, there are also principles and characteristics at work in the spiritual realm. One common characteristic is that demons do not announce their presence to others or to their victims. Demons do not want to be discovered and often are very angry when they are detected, as was the demon in Mark 1. In fact, a person usually remains unaware of their true condition until one of three things occurs to produce a change in the demon's incognito activity.

First: If a man or woman of God, who operates with authority in the spirit realm, comes in close contact with a demonized person, demons will be forced to manifest. This often occurred in Jesus' public ministry. It still happens today. I have seen demons manifest while I preached in a church service or taught in a small group, as evidenced in the following story.

Several years ago, I was preaching a series of messages in a church. On the second evening, a group of rebellious young people came into the church and sat down. As I preached, they began to mock me, making all kinds of facial expressions and hand gestures, becoming loud and disruptive. My natural tendency would have been to rebuke them, but the Holy Spirit restrained me. When I closed the message and offered an invitation for salvation and deliverance, most of the young people left, but three came forward. After hours of debate, these three submitted their lives to Jesus Christ as Lord and several demons were cast out of them. Later, we discovered that these young people belonged to a group of Satan worshippers.

Second: The demonized person may begin to suspect demonic activity is causing some of his personal problems. This often occurs when a person attends a seminar or begins to receive specific teaching about how the demonic kingdom works.

Third: If the demon takes so much control in the person's life that the victim becomes emotionally, spiritually, or physically injured and incapacitated, it may become obvious what is happening to the person. The following story illustrates how demonic activity can become evident in a person's life.

STORY OF TWO BROTHERS

One day, a woman telephoned me saying, "I have two children that I can no longer keep in school because of their anger and behavior. Would you please see them?" As she drove her children to Dallas, they fought in the car, not getting along for a minute. When they arrived, I listened intently as the mother described their problem.

She explained that the boys, aged six and nine, would go into rages and destroy their classroom, breaking things, pulling hair, screaming, yelling, and disrupting the whole class. Then, suddenly they would "snap out of it" and have no memory of anything that had happened.

The first-grader would say to his mother, "I don't want to do things like this, but something comes over me and I can't stop it. I do bad things." The mother said, "My two boys cannot play together without fighting. Sometimes they attack each other viciously, hurting each other. My youngest son cannot sit still for a moment. He is constantly in motion, touching, pulling, continually putting his fingers on things or in his mouth. He even chews his fingernails to the quick until they bleed. He has been diagnosed by doctors and the school as having ADD, Attention Deficit Disorder." A spirit of torment seemed to operate through this child. Their doctor's solution was to keep him on strong medications, which made him act like a zombie.

The children had been expelled from three private schools and two public schools. The school officials said the boys could not come back to school unless the mother could assure the school her sons' behavior had changed.

After talking with the mother, it was obvious the boys were suffering from an ancestral curse of anger. Their father, who worked out of town, was away for long periods of time. He didn't have much of a relationship with his wife or his children. The boys not only felt deeply

25

rejected because of his absence, but their father had a tremendous problem with anger which the children had inherited.

We prayed together and closed the doors to Satan in each of their lives. We broke the ancestral curses and the children gave their anger to God, who miraculously set them free. Immediately, the youngest boy stopped his hyperactivity and sat calm and peacefully. He quietly said, "Mother, it is all gone."

When she returned home, the mother called and said, "Our six-hour trip home was wonderful. There was no fighting and no hyper-activity. Today my sons are playing and working together in our home."

If Jesus left the synagogue in Capernaum and went throughout Galilee preaching and casting out demons in other synagogues (Mark 1:34, 39), why should we expect our condition to be any different today? Jesus addressed a demonic spirit of infirmity in a woman who had suffered for eighteen years and was bowed over, unable to straighten up (Luke 13:11-16). Today, we would probably say she had osteoporosis or some kind of crippling arthritis. Yet when the demon was cast out of the woman, she was immediately healed, evidenced by her back straightening up. Jesus called her a "daughter of Abraham," which meant that she was a believer. Also in Luke, Jesus rebuked the fever in the disciple Peter's mother-in-law, who was unable to get up from her bed (Matthew 8:14-15) and she was healed. She was also a believer.

DEMONIC ACTIVITY IN THE CHURCH!

Have you ever been guilty of lies, hypocrisy, deception, scheming, or pride since becoming a Christian? In the Book of Acts, Ananias and Sapphira apparently conspired together to sell land and give a portion of its sale price to the church, but tell the apostles they had given it all. They chose to cooperate with the lies and scheming of Satan that had filled their hearts.

At this time in history, the church was in unity and its membership lovingly cared for one another. They shared all things in common—the wealthier members sold land and possessions and gave the money to the church to care for those less fortunate. Barnabas had sold a tract of land, brought the money and laid it at the apostles' feet.

The attention given to Barnabas over this extravagant gift evidently disturbed Ananias and Sapphira. While Barnabas was occupied with the needs of others, Ananias and Sapphira were preoccupied with their own "felt needs." They needed to be part of "the group" in the church.

So, Ananias and Sapphira sold a possession and kept back part of the money. His wife, who was privy to it, brought a portion of the sale and laid it at the apostles' feet. But Peter asked Ananias why Satan had filled his heart to lie and to keep part of the proceeds from the sale of the land (Acts:5:1–3). The word "fill," which is translated in the Greek as *pieroo,* means "to make full," indicating that it was someone or something other than Ananias which filled his being. In order for this presence to fill Ananias, he had to desire its presence and welcome its lies. His deception was a willful act and because he persuaded his wife to agree with him, she, too, became part of the lie. Letting your heart be filled requires a voluntary action of agreement. Sadly, many churches today are full of people, who like Ananias and Sapphira, are controlled by their felt needs. They practice deception because their hearts are filled with lies.

Once I ministered to a Christian lady who was a faithful church member. She sang in the choir, worked with the children, and over the years was hailed as one of the most dedicated teachers in the congregation. She came to me under heavy guilt and depression. She explained that she was from a long line of people who had been faithfully serving the Lord and His church. When she received ministry, it was revealed that she had had an affair with a pastor years ago and was continuously plagued by desires of lust and adultery. Through her own wrong choices and disobedience, the enemy had gotten his hook into her and had harassed her for years. She was set free and is no longer harassed by those demons.

PAUL'S ADVICE CONCERNING SATAN

The apostle Paul gave instructions concerning servants of the Lord—men and women of God—to be careful less they find themselves captured by Satan.

> *And the servant of the Lord must not strive; but be gentle unto all men, apt to teach, patient. In meekness instructing those that oppose themselves if God peradventure will give them repentance to the acknowledging of truth. And that they may recover themselves out of the snare of the devil, who are taken captive by him to do his will—2 Timothy 2:24–26.*

Paul is clearly declaring that a believer's will can be taken captive by Satan. The term "recover themselves" in the Greek means "may return to soberness." Similar to intoxication, the devil's method is to numb the conscience, confuse the senses, and paralyze the will. Satan is the intoxicator and captivator of men's minds, with the final purpose being to control and manipulate the servants of God into doing his will instead of the Father's.

Have you ever lost your temper? Have you ever experienced hating someone or falling into deep depression? Maybe you have even had thoughts of suicide. The truth is that demons can have great influence and control over any area of a believer's life to which he is given access.

In summary, even Spirit-filled believers can be affected by demonic activity. The young minister at the beginning of this chapter came under Satan's control when a door was opened in his life through childhood molestation and abuse. Once the door was opened, the spirit of whoredom entered in and the young man became hooked on pornography and perverted sex. His own choices then compounded the ancestral curse which had initially opened the door.

As Christians we can be demonized—controlled, manipulated, and opposed by evil spirits. An evil spirit cannot own us, because we are owned by Jesus. We have been bought with the blood of Jesus Christ, and we belong to Him. The paradox in the life of the believer is that although we have been translated into the Kingdom of Light, we can still allow the kingdom of darkness to rule in many areas. The believer must have the chains cut and the enemy's hold broken, so he or she can walk continually in the light.

And the God of peace shall bruise Satan under your feet shortly—Romans 16:20.

CHAPTER 3

A Fixed Fight

The conflict in the universe centers on who will have authority—God or Satan. These two forces are always at work—God and His legitimate authority, Satan and his host of rebellious forces. It's an age-old battle between good and evil, light and darkness. Spiritual warfare exists. But you cannot begin to fight the darkness until you understand who it is that you are fighting and why the battle started in the first place.

THE AUTHORITY OF GOD

God's throne is established on His authority. All things were created, and the laws of the universe are maintained, through this self-existent divine authority system. The archangel Lucifer became Satan when he usurped God's dominion. By competing with God, he became God's adversary. Satan's desire to set his throne above the throne of God violated the divine authority structure. Self-exaltation was the culprit; rebellion was the cause.

Satan's hostility against us today is the direct result of our attributing authority to God. When we violate God's authority, we are, in essence, submitting to the dark principles of rebellion. Satan is still a usurper today. He doesn't care how much we preach or teach or whatever we might choose to do in the church. Satan is not afraid of our prayers, Bible study, fasting, Scripture-quoting, or confession as long as self-exaltation reigns in our hearts! His only fear is when we submit ourselves to God's authority.

Our entire relationship with God is regulated by whether or not we've acknowledged His sovereignty—whether we've bowed our knee to Him. Before we can work for God, we must submit to Him. Each of us at some point in our Christian journey must encounter the authority of God, be broken into submission, and learn to live in obedience to Him.

THE BIRTH OF THE CONFLICT

Man was created and fashioned by God for relationship. When Adam was formed by God's own hand, he was given dominion, command, and jurisdiction over the earth and its resources. God not only placed all the created things on the earth under the authority of Adam, giving him dominion over them, but He also placed Adam under His authority that Adam might learn obedience. God's bequest of dominion over the earth was a genuine gift. Dominion over the earth lawfully became man's right, and how he used it became his responsibility.

The great battle between light and darkness, the truth and the lie, began as Satan approached Eve with his questioning of God's words. "...Hath God said ye shall not eat of every tree in the garden?" (Genesis

3:1). The serpent's question enticed Eve to open the door, and Satan rushed in with doubt and unbelief. He even manipulated Eve into adding to what God said! (See Genesis 3:3.) God told Adam and Eve to not eat the fruit of the tree. Eve added touch to the command. Once Satan had convinced Eve that she could touch the fruit without consequence, he could easily entice her to eat.

The truth always leads to freedom, the lie to bondage. When Adam chose to obey Satan, to follow his principle of rebellion rather than submission to the authority of God, he became Satan's slave. And as a slave, Adam lost his legal rights, not only to his person but to his domain. Adam had unwillingly handed over that gift of dominion to Satan. Satan became "the ruler of this world" with legal authority to rule over man.

By eating the forbidden fruit in disobedience and rebellion, Adam and Eve found a source of right and wrong in something other than God Himself. Ever since, disorder has prevailed in the world. Man still operates under the illusion that he is able to discern good from evil on his own, apart from God.

Adam and Eve, who had been created to walk in intimate relationship with God, now hid from Him. Fear, which they had never known before, possessed them. Peace was gone. They now ran from rather than to their Creator. Guilt and shame replaced purity and transparency, and death entered their spirits.

GOD'S REDEMPTIVE PLAN

Without a doubt, the all-powerful God who rules the cosmos had the power to nullify Satan's subjugation of Adam and his legacy. However, such actions by God would have disregarded His own system of justice. If Satan's dominion was to be annulled, a strategy had to be found to ransom humanity and reclaim Adam's forfeited authority. It had to be a strategy that would not transgress God's own governmental principles. Since Satan had become the authentic master of Adam and the lawful "god of this world," the Lord would not arbitrarily revoke his claim. God would not violate His own character and ethics, not even to redeem mankind from Satan. No other created being would be able to enter into combat for Adam's forfeited inheritance and jurisdiction. These legal rights were never given to the angels, nor were they lost by angels. Since the rulership of the earth had been delegated to man and consequently lost by man, it had to be lawfully restored by a man. How could this possibly happen? Every descendent from Adam was born in Adam's likeness and thus was born under the dominion of Satan. Hence, only an authentic human being, who was not a part of Adam's rebellion and therefore not Satan's slave, must be found for this noble purpose.

For the human intellect, the circumstances appeared impossible, but God, who finds a way when there is no way, found a way to solve the dilemma.

But when the fullness of the time was come, God sent forth his Son, made of a woman, made under the law, to redeem them that were under the law, that we might receive the adoptions of sons. And because ye are sons, God hath sent forth the Spirit of his Son into your hearts, crying Abba, Father! Wherefore thou art no more a servant, but a son, and if a son, then an heir of God through Christ—Galatians 4:4–7.

God's divinely brilliant solution was the incarnation. When the Holy Spirit of God overshadowed and impregnated Mary, God became man in the person of Jesus. He had a divine, sinless nature over which Satan had no right nor sway. Yet as the son of Mary, He was qualified as a part of the human race to enter the legal contest to restore Adam's forfeited inheritance.

Thus, our redemption required the imperative of the virgin birth. The first Adam was created without a mother, and the second Adam was born without an earthly father. If Jesus had been Adam's descendant, He would have been born under the authority of Satan. But He was born the Son of God and Satan had no legal right to Him.

If Jesus had sinned, He would have been disqualified to challenge Satan. He had to be tested and found morally spotless and spiritually flawless. Satan's strategy and master plan was to incite Him to rupture fellowship with His father, to coerce Jesus to rebel and move independently—to decide right from wrong on His own. Throughout His earthly life, this was the contest between Jesus and the lord of darkness.

THE BATTLE RAGES

The future hopes and dreams of the entire world and all mankind would be determined by the results of this battle. If Satan could with overpowering temptation seduce Jesus into thinking just one thought outside the will of His heavenly Father, he would remain the conqueror and all humanity would be conquered. Although Jesus was indeed God, He had to enter and win this contest as a descendant of Adam—a man. Jesus, the Son of God, did have at His disposal all the power of heaven, but He matched Satan in a human body the same as ours. In this body He was subjected to every common temptation and yet overcame them all.

From Jesus' birth to His resurrection, the contest intensified with raging fury. In this divine plan for recovery of what the "first Adam" had lost, the "Last Adam", Jesus, and "the serpent" faced off in a destiny determining struggle. For thirty-three years the storms of the battle grew unabated. The deposed Lucifer, the former archangel who sang as the cosmos was being created, called forth all the resources of the underworld to support his all-out attack upon the man Jesus. Surely one flaw could be laid open, one evil intent, one rebel action, one selfish attitude disclosed, and the Father's ingenious plan to redeem mankind from slavery would be forever thwarted.

The evil rebel of darkness used every means of demonic warfare available, from the deaths of the children in Bethlehem to Jesus' temptation in the wilderness. From the hateful determination of the Pharisees to the excruciating pressure in the Garden of Gethsemane, it continued. From the calculated betrayal of Judas to the horrendous beatings by the Romans and finally the ignominious death on the cross, Satan tried to pry Jesus' loyalty away from His heavenly Father and over to him.

In the wilderness, Satan suggested a means by which Jesus could recover rulership of the world and bypass the cross—just fall down and worship him. Again and again Jesus answered his demonic suggestion perfectly with scripture, "It is written." But never did He challenge Satan's assertion that the kingdoms of this world were legally Satan's to give. He knew that He could redeem all men from Satan's slavery only by paying in full for mankind's rebellion and sin.

The contest which had originally begun in the heart of Lucifer and first touched Earth in the Garden of Eden reached its full passion in the Garden of Gethsemane. "And being in agony He prayed more earnestly: and His sweat was as it were great drops of blood falling down to the ground" (Luke 22:44). The dark burden upon Him was so excruciating that it brought blood drops through the pores of His brow. Jesus the son of God, holy, pure, and undefiled, was facing the reality of being made sin. He would become so utterly identified with sin that His Father would not only turn His face away from Him, but would pour out upon Jesus His wrath against sin. As Jesus, in agony, uttered the words, "Not my will, but thine be done" (Matthew 26:39), recovery of man's God-given destiny was determined and assured.

THE CONFLICT WON!

As Jesus submitted to death on the Cross, bowed His head and released His spirit without even one small defeat or failure, Satan's fate was sealed. When Jesus died without once rebelling against the Father, He vanquished Satan. All of Satan's legal claims upon the earth and the entire human race were canceled. The war was won!

Jesus Christ had disarmed and dethroned the adversary of mankind. He burst forth victoriously from the bowels of death. Christ alone had become the scapegoat for the sin of the whole world, as if He Himself were guilty of the entirety of that sin. As His soul was made an offering for sin, He had to "descend into hell" (Ephesians 4:9). The Father had to pour out the full force of His wrath against sin upon His beloved Son. This act demonstrates the infinite value God places on obtaining, not only a family of His very own, but also a bride for His Son.

Christ, resurrected in a human body, ascended into the heavens and sat down at the right hand of the Father proving conclusively that Satan's bankruptcy was complete. Jesus "took the teeth out of" demonic powers and made an open show of them by triumphing over them. Hell was thrown into total chaos! Satan was stripped of his usurped legal authority over mankind. His dominion over the earth was snatched. From this climactic struggle with the underworld of darkness, Jesus emerged triumphant with the keys to death and hell. Furthermore, Jesus translated us from the kingdom of darkness into the Kingdom of Light (Colossians 1:12-13).

SAINTS IN THE LIGHT

The purpose of this mighty conflict was to restore man to fellowship, authority, and dominion. When Jesus stormed forth from the dark abyss of death and ascended into the heavenlies, all believers were raised and seated together with Him! Every believer is completely identified with Christ from Calvary to the ascension.

> *But God, who is rich in mercy, for his great love wherewith He loved us, Even when we were dead in sins, hath quickened us together with Christ by grace ye are saved; and hath raised us up together, and made us sit together in heavenly places in Christ Jesus—Ephesians 2:4–6.*

According to Scripture, we are crucified with Him, buried with Him, raised with Him, exalted with Him, and enthroned with Him (Romans 6). This is possible because each person can trace their human seed back to Adam. In Adam, we rebelled and sinned against God. Through a new birth, we were born again and we became the seed of Jesus. Therefore, when Jesus died, overcame Satan, arose from the dead, and ascended to the right hand of the Father, we were in Him. We became victors—champions—saints in the Light!

Scripture says we are "bone of his bone, flesh of his flesh." (Genesis 2:23). In Him, when He subjugated the troops of darkness and left them unarmed and disabled, we who believe were participants in that triumph. When He seized the keys of death and hell from Satan and burst forth from that dark prison, we shared that victory. When He ascended on high and took His seat in the heavenlies, we were exalted with Him. Even now, we are so much a part of Him that we are called the body of Christ (1 Corinthians 12:27).

Therefore, Satan no longer has power over us. Instead, we have been given authority over him! God's authority on the earth has been restored. As we submit to Jesus Christ, His authority is ours. Remember, Jesus did not defeat Satan for Himself. He did it for us!

THE ROARING LION TODAY

If Jesus really defeated Satan, why does the earth seem to be covered with sin, violence, and injustice rather than love, joy, and peace? Why does Satan continue to exercise such power on earth? There are several reasons.

First: Ignorance! Too many believers in the church do not fully understand that they have been liberated! Jesus returned to heaven, gave the authority and dominion to believers, and sent His power to us through the Holy Spirit. Yet many in the church are steeped in unbelief.

Second: Satan is a sore loser. He does not concede without a fight. He is contentious and does not surrender one inch of ground until he is forced to do so! Believers need to realize they have the upper hand and then stand firm in faith until they experience the victory. When we stand in the name and authority of Jesus, Satan has no choice but to flee!

Third: When Satan throws dark clouds of doubt and despair over our minds and hearts, we seem to easily forget that we are no longer subject to Satan's authority. Therefore, we allow him to intimidate, harass, and oppress us. We lose sight of the fact that we are actually a part of Christ's body and as such, we have been given authority over all the enemy's power. We thoughtlessly lapse back into old mindsets of fear and defeat, seeing ourselves as we once were in Adam and not as we are today in Christ. Satan knows that he lost. However, he still carries on guerrilla warfare against the church through use of trickery, deception, intimidation, and fear.

Fourth: Even though God could put Satan completely away, He wants us to have on-the-job training in overcoming! Just as a weightlifter trains and develops strength by overcoming the resistance of weights, we, grow stronger each time we resist the enemy (2 Timothy 2:2–5).

CHRIST'S VICTORY WAS FOR US!

Christ didn't conquer Satan for Himself. His entire substitutionary work at Calvary was for His bride, the church. Everything He did, He did for us. The old person we once were in Adam died! Our identification in Christ's death sets us free from sin, self, the Law, the world, and Satan!

Sins:
For I delivered unto you first of all that which I also received, how that Christ died for our sins according to the Scriptures—1 Corinthians 15:3.

Self:
I am crucified with Christ: nevertheless I live; yet not I, but Christ liveth in me; and the life which I now live in the flesh I live by the faith of the Son of God, who loved me, and gave himself for me—Galatians 2:20.

The Law:
But now we are delivered from the law, that being dead wherein we were held; that we should serve in newness of spirit, and not in the oldness of the letter—Romans 7:6.

The World:
But God forbid that I should glory, save in the cross of our Lord Jesus Christ, by whom the world is crucified unto me, and I unto the world—Galatians 6:14.

Satan:
Ye are of God, little children, and have overcome them: because greater is he that is in you, than he that is in the world—1 John 4:4.

As you resist the enemy, remind yourself constantly of who you are—a child of the Most High God. Jesus has given you the keys to the Kingdom of Heaven, but He does not force you to use them. He intercedes for you and waits for you to take action. The rest is up to you. You cannot do what He has done. He will not do what He had commanded you to do. Jesus Christ has left the enforcement of Calvary's victory in your hands.

We must continually renew our minds with Scripture (Romans 12:2) that reinforce our new identity in Christ. Satan wants us to forget that we are risen and exalted with Christ, that we are united with Christ on the throne, and that all demonic enemies are under our feet.

When we find ourselves in bondage to demons of fear, rejection, sickness, immorality, or sins and limitations of any kind, it is often because we are ignorant of what Christ accomplished on our behalf. Individually, we must assume the responsibility to lay down the satanic principle of rebellion, submit ourselves completely to God, and use our God-given weapons to take back the land Satan and his demonic forces have stolen from us. He is a usurper. He has no legal right. The fight is fixed. We have already won!

PART 2

THE 2-5-14 STRATEGY:
2 WAYS OF ACCESS
5 OPEN DOORS
14 ROOT SPIRITS

CHAPTER 4

BLINDSIDED BY INTRUSION

The schemes of the demonic realm affect your life. Have you ever felt as if a cloud was hanging over your head or a dark shadow was following you? Maybe it seemed as if there was an invisible barrier keeping you from what you really want to do or become. If so, it's time to sharpen your spiritual sight and realize there is more in this life than what can be seen!

For example, if you are a Christian, chances are you have at some time in your life experienced an attack or a temptation from Satan. In your heart, you knew what was happening. You could "see" it with your spiritual eyes. But you may not have understood how to withstand it, or why that particular thing happened on that particular day. Without a proper understanding of the spiritual world, you were engaged in a fight for which you had not been trained.

You may wonder how you could ever hope to learn to stand

against an invisible adversary. Take heart. You're not required to fight a blind match for which there are no rules! There are spiritual laws that operate in the universe, and Satan himself must play by the rules. For example, you have probably experienced an attack from Satan at a time when you were distant from the church or Christian friends. You were walking in a vulnerable place and suddenly an ungodly thought or temptation came to you. A situation just happened to occur that made it easy to sin.

Did you know that a lion will never attack an animal that remains within the herd? The lion will follow a herd and wait for an animal to be separated out. It may be an older animal who cannot keep up the pace, or it may be a young animal that wanders off or becomes separated from its mother. Or it may be one that just gets curious and wanders a little distance away from the others. That's when the lion attacks. As in the animal kingdom, when you allow yourself to be separated from fellow believers for whatever reason, you will become vulnerable to attacks from Satan, the roaring lion (1 Peter 5:8).

All of us have and will experience Satan's devouring attacks in our lives. But we can learn his devious ways and withstand his attacks. A significant spiritual principle to understand about how darkness operates: Satan can gain access into your life by intrusion or by legal ground.

INTRUSION

Satan always attacks anything that will affect the outcome of God's purpose for our lives. Have you noticed how Satan tries to interrupt your life by causing disturbances or unnecessary conflicts? He is a master at interruptions and distractions. His intrusions can cause you to miss much of what God really intends for your life.

Webster's definition of intrusion is "the act of pushing or thrusting in; the act of putting or coming in without being asked or wanted." Intrusion is any occasion in which Satan shoots his fiery darts or throws his "low blows" into your life. He runs in, does his little thing, and then runs away. You have not given him a just cause or reason to have access into your life. He has intruded and has no right to be there.

When He created mankind in His own image, God intended to be in continual communion with us, as He was with Adam and Eve before the fall. Therefore, Satan hates it when man worships and communes with God. He will always try to interrupt that fellowship with God by intruding into our lives, disrupting our focus on God, and causing us to focus instead on our difficult or distressing circumstances.

The difference between intrusion and legal ground (covered in the next chapter) is that intrusion always comes from the outside, never from the inside. Demonic attacks from the outside attempt to distract us, turn our thoughts in another direction, entice us to accept another philosophy, or even to look at something from a perspective other than God's. We have no control over an intrusive attack or over how or when it will come, because unlike attacks on legal ground, the source is not from within us.

Satan's intrusive "punches" should always be expected, but in keeping with his character or lack thereof, Satan doesn't always wage a frontal attack. He throws his sneaky punches from the side or from the rear to distract you from God's purpose for your life. To illustrate, a few years ago, a young man in his forties came to me for help. While in his early twenties, he had experienced a call of God upon his life and was preparing for ministry. During his seminary days, he had received an idea in the night about how to make a lot of money in order to "really serve God." By age forty five, he was engaged in a money-making business, with no time for ministry and little time for God. His dream of being a pastor was crowded out by the desire to make money. Satan came in through the back door, threw a sneaky punch, and distracted his focus from God's higher calling in this businessman's life.

Satan's goal is to destroy you, to bring you down, to keep you in the dark, to make you ineffective. If he can keep you ignorant of his game, then you will be less than God created you to be. You will spend your life fighting with one hand tied behind your back, in bondage in many areas of your life, uninformed or misinformed about the kingdom of darkness...unaware that you are even engaged in a fight!

SATAN'S STRATEGIES

Satan uses five primary strategies to defeat the believer with intrusion: lies and deception; accusations and condemnation; doubt, unbelief, and fear; the battle of the mind; and attack against the Word of God.

Strategy 1: Lies and deception. One day I made a statement to a lady who had sought my counsel, and it totally changed her life. She came to me for counsel. She was very angry as she explained her pain, saying, "I was molested by my father. All of my family knew about it, and nobody did anything. Until I left home at age eighteen, I was subjected to sexual abuse. Why did God let this happen to me?" She demanded, "If God is God, why couldn't He have kept this from happening? Why didn't He keep me safe? Why didn't He protect me?"

I said to her, "God is a man of His Word. He does not lie. Do you believe that?" She answered quietly, "Yes." I continued, "God said He did not protect you because of the sins of your ancestors. Your ancestors did not love God enough to worship and serve Him because they loved themselves and their sins. God said in His Word that He would visit the sins of them that hate Him to the third and fourth generation. What was done to you was done because of the sins of your

48

ancestors and not because God wasn't big enough to stop it."

She said to me, "I've been mad at the wrong person all these years, haven't I?" My answer to her was, "Yes! You've been mad at God, and it was not God's fault. The culprit is not God. The culprits are sin and Satan. God loves you so much that He made provision for your freedom and wholeness." That revelation changed her life.

Strategy 2: Accusations and condemnation. Has the devil ever said to you: "You're no good. You're sorry. You're worthless. You're shameful. Nobody wants you. You'll never get married. You'll never have a family. You're just a piece of garbage." If he has, remember; that is not what God's Word says!

Most people let the enemy bring them down because they do not know that they are righteous! "For He hath made him to be sin for us, who knew no sin; that we might be made the righteousness of God in him" (2 Corinthians 5:21).

In the middle of an early morning prayer meeting, I was prompted by the Holy Spirit to stop and give a brief teaching on righteousness and holiness. I looked out across the congregation and said to a lady, "You are as righteous as God." She said to me, "Oh, no! I'm not!" I said to her, "Then you are not saved." She said, "Yes, I am saved. I know I'm saved!" I said to her, "Then you are as righteous as God." "Well, that can't be," she replied, "because I got mad at my husband last night and we had a big fight. And last week I did this and the week before I did that...." I said to her, "None of that has anything to do with your righteousness. You don't know who you are in Jesus." When she saw that she was made righteous because God had given her His righteousness, it totally changed her life!

Perhaps you did "fall" yesterday, but that has nothing to do with your righteousness, or your "right standing" before God at this moment. Righteousness is a gift from God that is received by faith

(Romans 5:17–19). Righteousness is an absolute. Holiness is a progression. I am working on my holiness. I am learning to be more holy. I am seeking to be more like Jesus in every action and thought. But I am absolutely righteous.

Do not listen to the devil's lies and condemnations against you. He may tell you that you don't pray enough, or that you don't read the Bible often enough. Tell him, "You are absolutely right, Satan. But Jesus has done all those things often enough, and He has given me His righteousness. Therefore, I don't have to worry about how much is enough. Forget your accusations and your condemnations. I don't receive any of them."

If you sin, however, you do need to repent before God. There's a difference between Satan's condemnations and your sin. If you sin, you must repent and turn from sin to God, thanking Him that Jesus has already forgiven and cleansed you.

Don't see yourself as sinful and condemned, or you will "live it out" and continue to walk in that sin. See yourself as having God's gift of righteousness, reflecting righteousness in increasing dimension.

Strategy 3: Doubt, unbelief, and fear. Have you been shot down by Satan because you don't have the faith to believe that God loves you enough to do something good for you? God heals everyone else, but not you. He supplies money for everyone else, but not you. God takes care of everybody else's marriage, but He hasn't taken care of yours. Do you fail to lift your shield of faith because you don't believe God loves you enough to provide for you? Do you fail to trust Him, not really believing God loves you enough to help you? Don't let the enemy defeat you with doubt, unbelief, and fear.

Strategy 4: The Battle of the mind. In your mind a battle rages between the Holy Spirit and Satan. Satan wants to control your mind, but don't let him. Do not let your mind run wild as Satan assaults you. Bring every thought into obedience, captive to Jesus Christ. God's Word says to take every thought captive and to pull down every high and lofty thing that exalts itself against the knowledge of God.

> *For though we walk in the flesh, we do not war after the flesh: For the weapons of our warfare are not carnal, but mighty through God to the pulling down of strongholds; Casting down imaginations and every high thing that exalteth itself against the knowledge of God, and bringing into captivity every thought to the obedience of Christ—2 Corinthians 10:3-4.*

You may worry about inappropriate or evil thoughts passing through your mind, but don't. You haven't sinned. Just bring those evil thoughts into captivity! Only when you hold onto thoughts, entertain them, pamper them, and encourage them have you sinned in your mind.

My friend, Peter Lord said to me one day, "Henry, do you know when you have let the sin of lust rule in your heart?" I said, "No, tell me." He said, "In Florida where I live, I do a lot of jogging. As I jog down the street there may be a nice-looking lady sunbathing wearing very few clothes. If I look at her and think, Wow, what a beautiful woman! I have not sinned. But if I jog around the block again to take another look, I have just sinned!"

When Satan shoots his wicked thoughts at you, whether they are thoughts of adultery, lust, self-pity, judgment, or jealousy, pull those thoughts down! Seize them and bring them captive to Jesus. If you don't do that, those thoughts will take root in you, and you will find yourself in bondage to sin.

Strategy 5: Attacking the Word of God. After Jesus was baptized by

John the Baptist, the Holy Spirit led Him into the wilderness where Satan tempted Him for forty days using God's Word! Each time Satan used Scripture to ensnare, Jesus countered with a rebuttal, "It is written."

Satan even tried to use the Word on Jesus by taking Scriptures out of context! (See Luke 4:9–11.) But Jesus refused to dialogue with Satan and said, "It is said, Thou shalt not tempt the Lord thy God" (Luke 4:12).

David, too, realized the power of God's Word when he wrote "Thy word have I hid in mine heart, that I might not sin against thee" (Psalm 119:11).

As a believer, you are equipped to handle the devil's intrusion in your life, but you must know how to resist these five types of intrusion. Avoid arrogance where Satan is concerned, because no one is a match for Satan on his own. He can only be challenged with the Word and the power of God!

HANDLING INTRUSION

When Satan starts hitting from the blind side, throwing sneaky punches your way, you can handle his wicked intrusions!

First: Continue to keep your eyes on God and not on the circumstances Satan has placed before you. Give God glory in every situation. We are instructed in Scripture to give thanks in every thing, "for this is the will of God in Christ Jesus concerning you" (1 Thessalonians 5:18).

Second: Investigate whether this is intrusion or whether you have given Satan access to your life through disobedience. You must receive instructions from God as to how to respond, rather than what the problem is at the present. Call upon God for His wisdom, power, and presence.

Third: Remember that people are not your enemies. If Satan cannot defeat you, he will often try to subdue someone whose anger will impact you. Often he tries to hinder or defeat a close family member or business associate. Satan uses our emotional ties to people whenever he can in order to cause a loss or disappointment or setback in our life.

Fourth: Glance at the problem only long enough to tell God about it, but do not become distracted by focusing on the problem. Satan's job is still the same as it was in the beginning—to break our communion with God. He was successful in intruding into the lives of Adam and Eve, inducing them to break communion with God. So when intrusion comes, look to God for His wisdom. Do not be consumed by the problem.

Fifth: Resist Satan and draw near to God. If we do that, Scripture says the devil will flee from us (James 4:7-8). Many people attempt to resist Satan without first submitting to God. In order to submit to God, you must do what God tells you to do. Submission is obedience. When you truly submit, you draw near to God and He draws near to you.

To resist Satan's intrusions, put on the whole armor of God (Ephesians 6:12-18). You have been given spiritual armor for the specific purpose of resisting Satan! We are instructed to take up the whole armor of God, not just part of it.

A TEENAGERS' STORY

While I was a pastor, a distraught parent called me saying, "Pastor, get over to my house. I don't have time to explain. Come quickly." Immediately I jumped into some clothes and sped across town. Walking into their kitchen, I discovered a fifteen-year-old young man with both wrists cut and bleeding. Remembering my Boy Scout first aid training, I ice-packed his wounds and stopped the bleeding. As I worked with his wounds, I began to question the wife. About that time her husband walked in the back door and said, "This is not the worst of it. There are three more in a drainage ditch out back."

He and I made our way through the darkness to a large concrete drainage ditch about ten feet deep, thirty feet long, and fifteen feet wide. In that ditch were three other young men about fifteen or sixteen years old. High on drugs and alcohol, they were raving out of their minds. When I jumped into the ditch and approached one of them, he began to curse and use all kinds of vulgar language. The father begged, "Please don't be offended; he does not mean this." The young man was this father's only son. As I pursued the teen, he turned and said, "I will kill you," and swung at me with his right fist. Catching his hands as he swung toward me, I crossed his arms and pushed him up against the side of the ditch.

About that time a very deep Asian-sounding voice came from the young man's mouth, saying, "I would kill you, but I can't. You always put on the armor of God!" When I took authority over the spirits and cast them out, the young man collapsed in my arms.

Many of us know about the armor, but we don't know how to put it on. It's much like a person in the military being issued a military weapon, but it is torn apart in front of him on a table. Technically, he has an automatic rifle, but does not know how to assemble it, so he can't use it to resist the enemy. Like the soldier, you may possess the parts of your armor, but you don't know how to put them together and place the armor on. So what is this spiritual armor and how do we put it on?

HELMET OF SALVATION

The helmet of salvation is your first piece of protection (Ephesians 6:17). Make sure you have established a saving relationship with Jesus Christ. A relationship with Christ is essential not only in fighting the battle, but in winning the war! Only through salvation can you claim the protection and power contained in the blood of Jesus. Never underestimate the power of His blood. It is by His blood that you were saved and redeemed, and it is by His blood that you can overcome the enemy.

BELT OF TRUTH

The piece of armor God has given us to combat Satan's lies and deception is the belt of truth (Ephesians 6:14). Jesus said, "I am the Truth." He didn't say, "I am part of the truth, or I am some of the truth." He is the Truth.

A tremendous fallacy in the western way of thinking is to equate intellectual assent to knowing the truth. Christianity then becomes a mental, cerebral experience. But knowing something in your mind does not mean you know it as the truth!

The word know in Scripture means "intimacy." If I have intimacy with the truth, the truth will set me free. And the Truth—all of the Truth—is Jesus. Anything contradictory to Jesus and the Bible is a lie.

BREASTPLATE OF RIGHTEOUSNESS

The next piece of spiritual armor to put on is the breastplate of righteousness (Ephesians 6:14). The breastplate of righteousness covers the vital organs of your body—the heart and the lungs. Satan brings accusations and condemnation to you about your past—some action, some sin you committed long ago—so you will submit to him and take off the breastplate of righteousness. When you take off the righteousness of Jesus, Satan can defeat you. Are you going out to war without your breastplate? If you do, you will be whipped, beaten, and possibly mortally wounded as Satan renders you useless to the kingdom of God.

How righteous are you? Are you 50 percent righteous? Ninety percent righteous? You probably believe you are somewhat less than 100 percent righteous, and need to work to obtain the rest. Truthfully, you are 100 percent righteous, because God's Word says you are. You are as righteous now as you ever will be because your righteousness is a gift from God. It is not produced by your good works, as religion would want you to believe. God gave you His righteousness as a gift when you were brought into the new birth experience, when you were born again.

PREPARATION OF PEACE

We are to walk on the path of peace (Ephesians 6:15). Not a path of frustration, anger, or hostility. Otherwise, how will others see that your life is different from theirs?

SHIELD OF FAITH

Above all, taking the shield of faith, wherewith ye shall be able to quench all the fiery darts of the wicked—Ephesians 6:16.

There were two kinds of Roman shields. One was a round shield, twelve to fourteen inches in diameter, and used in hand-to-hand combat. The other was called a "door shield" which was large enough for a person to hide behind. This human shield was made with one piece of light, solid wood and covered with animal skin which had been soaked in water. When the enemy shot his fiery darts at the person, the skin on the shield would put out the fire.

A "fiery dart" was an arrow tipped with tar or pitch and then set on fire. When a soldier took his bow and shot the flaming arrow, it would throw burning tar all over the person, as well as anyone else nearby. But if such a dart hit the door shield with the leather that had been soaked with water, the fire would be put out; the hot tar would be cooled. Soldiers would often lock their door shields together as they marched toward a city, creating a unified wall of protection.

The shield of faith that God has given us is like the soldier's door shield, protecting us from Satan's fiery darts. The weapon of faith is simply believing God and the promises contained in His Word. We have to believe and join our faith to what He has said. Remember, whatever you ask in Jesus' name, if you believe, you will receive (Matthew 21:22; Mark 11:24).

SWORD OF THE SPIRIT

Resist Satan's intrusion by using the sword of the Spirit, which is the Word of God (Ephesians 6:17). The Bible is a two-edged sword—the Word and the Spirit. It is by the power of the Holy Spirit that we are able to withstand the attacks of Satan.

Not by might, nor by power, but by my spirit, saith the Lord of hosts—Zechariah 4:6.

Don't just say to the devil, "I don't like you." He does not care whether or not you like him. To use the sword against Satan, you need to know God's Word! You must resist the devil according to the Word of God.

Tell him what Jesus said: "Get thee behind me, Satan" (Luke 4:8). Tell him to leave you alone because he has no right to you! Quote the Bible. Put on the whole armor of God because none of us are exempt from Satan's deceitful strategies! We must always be prepared for spiritual warfare.

HAVING DONE ALL, STAND

One day, I was ministering to a lady, and she said impatiently, "How long is this going to take?"

"However long it takes for all the enemy's strongholds to be broken," I replied.

"I hope not more than an hour or so," she said. Impatience will keep us from our victory. There is no such thing as being able to put a time definition on how long it takes to break an attack of the enemy. You just fight until you win!

Remember, if Satan knows you are on a time schedule, he will simply be stubborn and hold out as long as he can. But if he knows you are not on one, he will realize there is no point in resisting or fighting because he has nothing to gain! Demons seem to know whether or not you are willing to stand. Although they can put up a difficult fight, they will eventually flee.

> *Put on the whole armor of God, that ye may be able to stand against the wiles of the devil. For we wrestle not against flesh and blood, but against principalities, darkness of this world, against spiritual wickedness in high places. Wherefore take unto you the whole armor of God, that ye may be able to withstand in the evil day, and having done all, to stand—Ephesians 6:11–13.*

Be bold and courageous. Strengthen your ability to persevere. Take a bull-dog grip. Draw a line in the sand and declare, "This is a do-or-die fight." If you do not give up, you will win.

CONCLUSION

When it comes to intrusion, remember that the fight is fixed. As long as you keep fighting, you will win! When you resist the devil, there is no such thing as losing the war against intrusion.

You only lose when you quit. Satan does have the power to overpower us, but he does not have the authority to do so. Authority commands power. You must be tenacious, determined, persistent and relentless in your battle against the strongholds.

Remember, it's a fixed fight and the outcome has already been sealed. Read the last chapter of Revelation. We win! Keep this thought in mind: you can do all things through Christ Jesus who strengthens you (Philippians 4:13).

C H A P T E R   5

AN ADVERSARY IN YOUR CORNER

D o you ever feel as if the devil has a key to your front door? He walks in, does whatever he wants, and won't leave, even when you try to throw him out. If so, then it's time to take away the keys! To take back the keys, you must first determine how Satan gained entrance into your life. In spiritual terms, his access into your life is called "legal ground." Legal ground occurs when Satan has a right to be in your life because you or someone else in authority—your parents or someone in your ancestral line—have shaken hands and welcomed him in. In other words, even if you are seeking to live in obedience to the Lord, you may be paying the price for bad decisions made by your parents or even your ancestors!

The Bible tells us not to "give place to the devil" (Ephesians 4:27). The word "place" in the Greek is the word *topos*, which means a literal place or terrain. You are not to give Satan any terrain in your life. He cannot just come in whenever he decides, unless you have given him that right. If he does come in, it means you have given him legal ground.

Would you believe that many Christians give access to Satan—hand him the keys to the front door of their lives—in a variety of ways without realizing what they are doing? Having your palm read, studying astrology, going to a fortune-teller, reading tarot cards or your horoscope or even having them read for you, gives place to the enemy. Even horror movies, certain books, or some television shows, can open a door to Satan. You can also open your spirit to the kingdom of darkness through pornography, drugs, and addictive substances. In essence, whatever enslaves you becomes your master! Satan schemes to bring you under his control in order to legally do what he wishes in your life.

Giving Satan legal ground is like me going to a judge and obtaining a legal document that gives me the right to enter your home anytime I want, day or night. The judge orders you to give me a key to the front door so I will not have to force my way inside. I can come in at 2:00 a.m., wake you up, turn on the lights, scream, yell, beat on the walls, turn over the furniture, and make all kinds of trouble for you.

You call the police, but when they come, I simply show them my legal document from the judge. And because it says I have the legal right to be in your home, they can't do anything—not even ask me to leave the premises. However, if you went to the judge and asked him to rescind my rights to your home, he could legally rule that I no longer have a right to be there. Then, the next time I came into your house to cause trouble, you could call the police. When they arrive, I would show them my paper stating I have a legal right to enter your home. But when you show the police your document stating that my right has been taken away, the police will cart me away from your property and off to jail. My legal right of access has been taken away!

SAM'S STORY

Sam was born into what looked like an ordinary home, but it was totally void of love. His father believed his mother had conceived Sam while having an affair with another man. So Sam's father never fathered him. Sam was never held by his father. He never played with him or told his son that he loved him. Instead, Sam was ridiculed, physically abused, rejected, and humiliated throughout his childhood.

His mother turned to alcohol to cope with the hate and strife in the home. She would get drunk and would turn on Sam. His body had burn marks all over it from cigarettes. Even worse, his heart had deep emotional scars from hateful words spoken by his mother. She would tell him, "If you had never come along, I wouldn't be in this mess." Sam was made to believe that his parents' failed marriage was because he was born. Sam was blamed for everything that went wrong in the family.

They lived in a neighborhood torn by racial strife. As a little, white boy living in a predominately African-American neighborhood, Sam had to fight to defend himself. He learned to hate very early, not only his family, but other people as well. As a defense against the unbearable pain, Sam's heart became as hard as stone. He grew up hating his father, his mother, and the boys on the street who bullied him day after day. Yet one bright light existed in Sam's life. He lived a block from a church that extended love to neighborhood children. Since his Sunday school teacher showed him kindness and attention, Sam gave his heart to Jesus.

However, Sam came to see me after three broken marriages, drug addiction, and the death of one of his children. Having made a fortune and lost it all, Sam knew his life was hopelessly out of control. He was consumed with lust. He had several adulterous affairs, which along with his drug and alcohol addictions, had ended his three marriages. Sam's life was in shambles and he knew that he needed God to do the impossible for him.

For several hours, I led Sam in a process of forgiving his parents, his three ex-wives, and a long list of others. Sam then laid down the many prejudices he had carried in his heart. Together, we broke the many vows he had made against his mother and father. Sadly, it was those very vows that had spun him into a cycle of similar addictions and defeat.

We, then, dealt with ancestral curses in his life. Through prayer, we broke their power. After calling forth many root spirits and dealing with each of their fruit, I commanded them to leave Sam. Then, Jesus stepped in to heal Sam's broken heart and his life was forever changed.

RECLAIMING LOST GROUND

Satan has devised a method by which he gets access into our lives legally. He entices us to become enmeshed in the kingdom of darkness and until this "legal ground" is recovered, we cannot order him out.

Legal ground can only be recovered through genuine repentance. Many of us may feel sorry after we sin, but often we are not willing to turn from our sin. True repentance means feeling such regret over a past action or attitude that we change our mind and our actions. We turn away from sin and to obeying God.

God is not in the quick-fix business. He has already destroyed Satan's legal right to our lives through the Cross. When we choose to fellowship with darkness rather than light, we are choosing bondage rather than freedom. When you are willing to repent in your heart and turn away from sin, what is legally yours also becomes experientially yours.

Not long ago I was counseling a man who had AIDS. His mother insisted that I pray for him to be freed from these tormenting spirits. After he began sharing with me, he confessed that he was a homosexual and had contracted AIDS through his lifestyle of many years. I looked into the young man's eyes and asked, "Are you willing to repent of a lifestyle that has given Satan the legal right to come into your life?"

Sadly, he wasn't. He came at the request of his mother. Therefore, praying for his deliverance and healing would not have done any good because he was unwilling to repent from a lifestyle of rebellion (Romans 1:27).

Repentance means that you must hate the sin that has enslaved you. You must be sick of it, tired of serving it, and weary from having it rule your life. You must decide to turn away from doing it.

Often we do not want to call "sin" what God calls it. We want to give it a name that is more socially acceptable, such as a "sickness" or "disease." But when demonic forces take hold and bring you to the point of addiction, it is not merely a sickness or a disease. It is a bondage brought on by the enemy.

Freedom will not come until you repent and let God take away the enemy's legal ground that the demonic realm has in your life. You may control the form or extent of your addiction by your will, but you will not be able to break the stronghold. The bondage will remain in your life. It may be difficult to turn from your addiction because you are not tired enough of it. You may be tired of the results of it, but not tired enough of the addiction itself.

A few years ago, I was praying with a man about his troubled marriage. He was addicted to pornography, was having a sexual affair with another woman, and was being bothered by lustful thoughts. I asked if he was willing to repent of entertaining lust and letting adulterous thoughts control his mind, which set him up for adultery. But surprisingly, the man did not want to stop his sinful actions. He just wanted his marriage fixed.

Let's face it. You will never recover your legal ground until you are willing to repent for that which gave the darkness legal right to come in and occupy you. Many Christians want God to move in and "fix" some things in their life, but they do not want to genuinely repent, turn from their sin, and walk in a lifestyle of holiness and righteousness. Instead people want to "have their cake and eat it, too." We cannot sin and then somehow escape the consequences of sin. That will not happen. Praying for "crop failure" after sowing wild oats simply will not work.

The Father delights in showing mercy. The Holy Spirit rushes to our aid when we get down to business. When people are willing to repent, demons have no power to stand in the face of the Lord Jesus.

If we confess our sins, he is faithful and just to forgive us our sins, and to cleanse us from all unrighteousness—1 John 1:9.

The word confess means to "name as God names, to say the same thing." If we name sin as God does and are willing to turn from practicing it, God will cleanse us from all unrighteousness and Satan's legal ground will be recovered.

Remember how the enemy had access to Sam's life through legal ground—ancestral curses of divorce, alcohol addiction, and rejection were in operation, as well as word curses spoken against Sam by his parents. Because of all the pain and hurt, Sam became angry and made inner-vow judgments against his parents. He fell into the trap of sexual sin and addictions. But when he came to the end of his rope, Sam finally did what was necessary. He repented of his sin. He took back the legal ground and closed the doors to Satan. Sam walks in freedom today, thanks to the glorious power and love of Christ Jesus.

CHAPTER 6

FIVE OPEN DOORS

There are five open doors which invite the demonic forces of darkness into our lives. These doors are; disobedience (willful sin), unforgiveness, emotional trauma, inner vows and judgments, and curses. If one or more of these doors is open, Satan has legal ground to operate in your life.

DOOR 1: DISOBEDIENCE

Is disobedience an open door in your life? Disobedience is any action or attitude that Scripture tells you not to do or have, or anything Scripture tells you to do and you refuse to do it. Sins of disobedience are willfully chosen. They may be such a part of your life that they are habitual and seem a natural part of you.

A few years ago a man told me, "Each week, I work outside in all kinds of weather. I work hard for my money, and I am going to spend it the way I want. Every weekend I buy a case of beer, and I drink until I am drunk. That's my pleasure, that's my privilege, and I am going to do it because I want to." This man was willfully disobeying God, for Scripture states that we are not to get drunk. To be drunk, therefore, is a willful sin of disobedience.

Willful disobedience will lead you into bondage. It does not matter what the sin is; it will eventually capture your will. This is not accidental. It is Satan's design for you. Scripture says:

> *Know ye not, to whom ye yield yourselves servants to obey, his servants ye are whom ye obey; whether of sin unto death, or of obedience unto righteousness—Romans 6:16.*

DOOR 2: UNFORGIVENESS

Unforgiveness is a second door that may be open to provide satanic access into your life. Unforgiveness is refusing to let go of or excuse a debt owed by another person.

Many of us do not really understand the concept of forgiveness. We've been taught that forgiveness is a product of our mind or our will, but that's not true. It's a product of our soul and spirit. You may know that you are instructed to forgive, but you may not understand how to forgive.

Forgiveness is a supernatural ability given to us by God. In the Gospels, Peter said to Jesus:

> *Lord, how oft shall my brother sin against me, and I forgive him? till seven times? Jesus said unto him, I say not unto thee, until seven times; but, Until seventy times seven—Matthew 18:21.*

Mathematics can tell you this would mean forgiving a person 490 times. You may wonder if you should keep a list. After all, 490 times in a lifetime would allow you to count how many times someone has sinned against you. However, the grammatical Greek construction of this verse means we are instructed to forgive the same person 490 times for the same sin, on the same day! Jesus chose an almost impossible number to illustrate that we are to forgive someone as often as that person sins against us! Then He offered a parable to illustrate what forgiveness is all about:

> *Therefore is the kingdom of heaven likened unto a certain king, which would take account of his servants. and when he had begun to reckon, one was brought to him which owed him ten thousand talents. But forasmuch as he had not to pay, his lord commanded him to be sold, and his wife, and children, and all that he had, and payment to be made. The servant therefore fell down, and worshipped saying, Lord, have patience with me, and I will pay thee all. Then the lord of that servant was moved with compassion, and loosed him, and forgave him the debt. But the same servant went out, and found one of his fellow servants which owed him an hundred pence: and he laid hands on him, and took him by the throat, saying, Pay me that thou owest. And his fellow servant fell down at his feet, and besought him, saying, Have patience with me, and I will pay thee all. And he would not: but went and cast him into prison, till he should pay the debt. So when his fellow servants saw what was done, they were very sorry, and came and told unto their lord all that was done. Then his lord, after that he had called him, said unto him, O thou wicked servant! I forgave thee all that debt, because thou desiredst me: shouldest not thou also have had compassion on thy fellow servant,*

even as I had pity on thee? And his lord was wroth, and delivered him to the tormentors, til he should pay all that was due unto him. So likewise shall my heavenly Father do also unto you, if ye from your hearts forgive not everyone their trespasses—Matthew 18:23–35.

The servant owed the king a debt of 10,000 talents and was unable to pay it. Even in today's terms, the amount of that debt was enormous—$20.5 million. The servant would have had to live forty lifetimes and pay all the money that he earned during those lifetimes toward his debt in order to repay the king.

Strategy for Today: This is the scope of the debt that you and I would owe God for our sins! It was unpayable! But Jesus paid the debt Himself, freely forgave us, and let us go. By His compassion and mercy, He released us and canceled the debt. No one deserves forgiveness. Jesus freely gave His forgiveness, and freely we are to receive it. We are also to forgive others freely—even God and ourselves—from judgments!

Now this servant, who was excused of this extraordinary debt, found a fellow servant who owed him 100 pence. This would amount to about $12.50 today, a very small debt. But the servant had his fellow servant thrown into jail because he could not repay the debt immediately.

When the other servants saw the injustice being done to a fellow servant, they told the king. The king summoned the servant and rebuked him severely. Since the servant did not forgive as he had been forgiven, the king turned him over to the tormentors, which is referred to in Revelation as the devil.

God Himself is the one who turns a believer over to Satan to be tormented until the believer is willing to forgive his brother.

Jesus makes this very plain in the book of Matthew:

So likewise shall my heavenly Father do also unto you, if ye from your hearts, forgive not every one brother their trespasses—Matthew 18:35.

Jesus said it was "from his heart" that a man must forgive trespasses or sins against him. "Heart" is the word for spirit or inner man. It is in your spirit that you must forgive your brother.

You have two choices when someone does you wrong—to forgive or to harden your heart. If you do not forgive, you have chosen to harden your heart! You must let the offense go, release it, and tear up the due note!

Forgiveness is *not* an option. It is the primary mark of a Christian. You must consider the consequences and realize there is a price to pay for unforgiveness. Unforgiveness will cause you to embrace bitterness that will affect everyone around you and build a wall between you and God. Bitterness can even result in physical illness, because of the various chemical changes that take place in the body when you refuse to forgive.

My wife, Tina, was born with scoliosis of the spine which caused back pain. One day as John Wimber, founder of the Vineyard movement, was praying for her, the healing process started. But then he stopped praying and asked her if there were any areas of unforgiveness with members of her family, specifically with her brothers. Tina could remember nothing. He then mentioned her father. She suddenly began to cry and spurt out, "My dad did not attend my high-school graduation." She had been totally unaware of this open wound in her heart. She forgave her father, which opened the door for complete healing!

Forgiveness is impossible within ourselves. We cannot do it on our own. There may be deeply rooted hurts from our childhood that occurred before we had the ability to reason things out or knew how to forgive. We must make the choice to forgive, let it go, and then cry out to God for His power to release and forgive the offender.

Forgiveness is a supernatural act accomplished by the Holy Spirit working through us. Many Christians often rationalize and deceive themselves into thinking they have forgiven someone when they have done so from their head, not their heart.

Once while ministering to a woman, I asked if there was any unforgiveness present in her life. She said there was not. Since it is rare to find someone with absolutely no unforgiveness lingering inside them, I suggested that we ask the Holy Spirit to reveal anyone she might yet need to forgive. When we prayed, suddenly names began to appear in her mind of people she needed to forgive.

If forgiveness is incomplete, we may say things like, "I'll forgive him this time, but he had better not ever let it happen again." That is not forgiveness. That is probation! Or, "I just can't forget what he did to me." Or, "He really doesn't deserve to be forgiven, because he doesn't even act like he's sorry."

We must forgive as God has forgiven us. He removed our sins as far as the East is from the West and remembers them no more (Psalm 103:12). He did not put conditions on forgiving us, so we cannot put conditions on anyone we are to forgive.

Some of us may forgive, but decide never to have anything more to do with the person who hurt or offended us. That is not the way God forgives us. He forgives us, takes us in, makes us His very own, and wants to maintain constant fellowship with us. If you do not want to associate or fellowship with a person who has wronged you, you know you have not completely released what is in your heart toward them.

What about forgetting the hurt? If you have hurt me and I have forgiven you, then I must be willing to maintain some kind of relationship with you. It may not be possible to have the same kind of relationship, but some kind is necessary.

Most Christians want to forgive, but we have been taught from childhood to do it as a decision of the mind. While forgiveness does start with a decision, it must go much deeper.

Is the following scenario representative of how you were taught to forgive? Do you remember fighting with a brother or sister growing up? Perhaps your sibling hit you and you started crying loudly. Your mother intervened and lectured your sibling. She turned and told your sibling to apologize, and then turned to you and told you to forgive. Not wanting to incur any more of your mother's wrath, your sibling said through clenched teeth, "I'm sorry." Then, your mother turned to you and said, "Say that you forgive him." And through your tears, you offered forgiveness. Then, your mother told you to give each other a hug. However, let's be honest. Your sibling did not repent and you did not forgive. Often this is the way it is with us today.

Unforgiveness keeps the door open for the enemy and his tormentors to come into your life and torment you. They will do so until you are willing to forgive. Sadly, much misery and failure in the church and in households is a result of unforgiveness.

God has forgiven us completely, lifted away our sin, brought us into His family, shared His inheritance with us, and desires to spend eternity with us. We have the power and enabling of the Holy Spirit and the heart and nature of the Forgiver in us.

GOD AS JUDGE

Forgiveness is not always easy. How can someone easily forgive rape, murder, incest, or abuse. If we forgive, does that mean that we excuse the perpetrator?

Even in the most difficult situations, true forgiveness is possible when we realize that everyone is accountable to God. God is the judge and the avenger—not us. Realizing this truth will help us to release forgiveness to others. Only our pride and arrogance stand in the way of releasing forgiveness.

Finally to complete the forgiveness cycle, we must bless and pray for the person who has wronged us. This has very powerful results. Consider Jesus' words in the Sermon on the Mount when He said:

> *But I say unto you, love your enemies, bless them that curse you, do good to them that hate you, and pray for them that despitefully use you, and persecute you—Matthew 5:44.*

DOOR 3: EMOTIONAL TRAUMA

The third open door to demonic activity is the door of emotional trauma. These hurts are inner wounds caused by sudden physical injury or emotional shock. Emotional trauma causes lasting damage to the psychological, spiritual, or emotional development of a person.

There are two kinds of wounds and trauma: that which we had a part in causing (such as disobedience which resulted in a consequence of our sinfulness), and that which we had no part in causing (such as abuse, rape, or molestation).

One interesting point about trauma is that what may deeply hurt, wound one's spirit, or bring emotional trauma to one person may not traumatize another person in the same way. This is why two children in a family may experience an event together and only one of them is traumatized by its effects. Each of us are traumatized by different actions, events, and to various degrees. Although what happens to us in life is not under our control, our response to what happens is under our control.

One of the greatest causes of trauma today is divorce. There's no such thing as an amiable divorce. When you marry someone, promise to live with that person for the rest of your life, and then decide to break that vow and go your own way, you will hurt your spouse and your spouse will hurt you. If children are involved, they will be hurt also. Everyone involved is hurt—grandparents, aunts and uncles, and family friends. Today, our society is dealing with a generation of shattered and scattered lives because of divorce. Divorce tears at the very fabric of every life involved in the family unit.

Accidents, near-death experiences, fearful experiences of any kind, or death in a family bring deep trauma to people. Abuse, (physical, mental, or sexual), also causes deep wounds. Molestation devastates children. Muggings, rapes, and violence of all kinds bring trauma in varying degrees. Rejection, ridicule, domination and control—especially by parents—can cause deep, far-reaching pain in a human spirit.

Whatever its source, when trauma occurs in a person's life, healing must come. Part of Jesus's ministry was to heal the brokenhearted, as reflected in this passage of text:

The Spirit of the Lord is upon me, because he hath anointed me to preach the gospel to the poor; he hath sent me to heal the brokenhearted, to preach deliverance to the captives, and recovering of sight to the blind, to set at liberty them that are bruised—Luke 4:18.

Did you know that a bruise is caused by inner bleeding? The Lord obviously knew we were going to have many brokenhearted people in the church—people bruised by sin, by others, and by circumstances. Jesus came to set us free and to heal our bruised lives.

Unfortunately, many in the church look at emotional healing as something metaphysical or psychological, and not something needed in the church. However, the church is full of wounded people who should first seek their own healing before attempting to heal someone else. In order for the church to function together as a whole body, those who are wounded must be healed.

Trauma is so unique and so individualized that it is impossible to cover all of its many causes. But deep inside, you know if you have a wound in your spirit or if you have been deeply hurt. If so, you have experienced some type of trauma and you will need healing.

One day I was sitting with a group of pastors, sharing about an event that had transpired in my life. Someone had betrayed me and hurt me deeply. I said, "It seems that Satan has some kind of opening in my life."

Thinking the opening was unforgiveness, my friends questioned me if I had forgiven the person. "Yes," I responded. "I have forgiven them."

One of those present then asked, "Have you been healed of the hurt?"

"No," I replied.

"A wound in your spirit is a cause," he said. "If you give Satan a cause, he will take advantage of it and walk into your life." The person then quoted this passage of Scripture:

As the bird by wandering, as the swallow by flying, so the curse causeless shall not come—Proverbs 26:2.

76

Immediately, I realized that I had not been healed of the emotional and spiritual hurt that had transpired in that betrayal. I asked those pastors to pray for me, and that day God brought healing in my life concerning that issue.

Throughout our lifetime, the deep reservoir of inner hurt and pain is something that most of us have pushed down, stuffed in, and tried to keep the lid on. But no matter what we do, it will keep bubbling up and boiling over.

Because emotional trauma often occurs in childhood, it sets us on a course of attitudes and reactions, causing us to always wonder why we behave in certain ways. And although we've all been victimized to some degree, it's our choice whether or not to remain a victim. We are not responsible for the wrong deeds of someone else. But we are responsible for our response to them.

God wants to free us from emotional trauma and heal our broken hearts. Experiencing God's supernatural healing is essential to take away the enemy's ground in our lives.

DOOR 4: INNER VOWS AND JUDGMENTS

The fourth door of satanic access is the door of inner vows and judgments. An inner vow is a vow made early in life. It is made with deep emotion, often in response to a person, an experience, or a desire. It's a vow made to ourselves, not to God or another person. Inner vows are based on judgments that we make, most often as children, against our parents, caregivers, schoolteachers, or others in authority.

Once made, such vows are soon forgotten. However, an inner vow resists the normal maturing processes. You do not just grow out of it. Inner vows may lie dormant for years until the right situation acts as a trigger. Often buried in the past and forgotten, these inner vows bind us to a mind-set or course of action which is fleshly and prevents our emotional or spiritual development. When we become a believer and the Holy Spirit fills us, He is prevented from penetrating that area because we have not broken the vow. We are still operating, in that area, as if we are fully in control of our lives.

> *But I say unto you, Swear not at all; neither by heaven; for it is God's throne: Nor by the earth, for it is his footstool: Neither by Jerusalem; for it is the city of the great King. Neither shalt thou swear by thy head, because thou canst not make one hair white or black. But let your communication be, Yea, yea; Nay, nay: for whatsoever is more than these cometh of evil—Matthew 5:34–37.*

Inner vows open a door for the evil one to gain legal ground in our lives. One day, each of us will give account for every vow we make.

A grandmother once came to me seeking help. With tears in her eyes, she confessed that she was abused as a child and that she abused her three children. She was troubled by watching her adult children physically abuse her grandchildren. Often, she found herself abusing them, too. "I can't take it any longer. You must help me," she begged.

I asked her to share about her childhood abuse. She was the third of six children. Whenever one child did something wrong, her father punished all six of them. He took them into the kitchen, stripped off their clothes, doubled up a twelve-foot extension cord, and began beating them until each stood in a pool of blood.

When she was ten years old, she made an inner vow. She promised herself that "If I ever have any children, I will never do to them what Daddy does to us." While she didn't punish them in the exact same way, she beat her children with whatever was at hand—a garden hose, a wooden spoon, a coat hanger, a belt, whatever she could grab up. In a fit of rage, she would beat her children.

Quickly I saw that the vow she had made had imprisoned her and set her on a track that she could not get off simply because she had judged her father. When she repented of her inner vow and asked God to forgive her for judging her father, freedom came. We broke the vow and its results ceased.

A few months later, she called to say it was working. "I have kept my grandchildren through every major holiday, two weeks at Christmas, and did not abuse them once," she shared with excitement. "I have even led one of my sons in breaking the same vow he had made against me, and my son has stopped abusing his children. I have two more sons to go, but it's working."

Child abuse is repeated from generation to generation because it is almost impossible for the abused child not to speak a vow of judgment against his or her abuser. The sin is then locked in to be perpetuated to the next generation and so forth—unless the vow is broken. That is why Scripture says:

> Judge not, that ye be not judged. For with what judgment ye judge, ye shall be judged: and with what measure ye mete, shall be measured to you again—Matthew 7:1–2.

The power of a vow! Even a seemingly good vow will bind you to a track, a fleshly course of action, that you cannot escape until the vow is broken. The power of the Holy Spirit cannot be released into the situation because of the vow which is based on the strength of the flesh! Vows have powerful implications.

A father may tell a child when he falls down, skins his knee, or hurts himself in some other way, "Get up. Dust off your jeans. Stop that crying! Boys don't cry! Suck it up and be a man!" The child swallows his tears, sucks in his feelings, puts a smile on his face, winces at the pain, and goes on. Years later, he wonders why he has no compassion for others in the church who hurt themselves or who are experiencing pain. His callous reaction is evidence that a vow is operative in his life.

Have you ever wondered why many men do not talk to their wives? Consider this scenario: a young man has done something wrong. His mother knows that he has done something wrong, and she says to him, "Tell me what you have done. I won't spank you." So she coaxes him into telling her the secret of his heart. Once the secret is divulged and the mother knows all the details, she lectures or disciplines him. Then, she holds it over his head and never seems to forget.

Quickly he learns and says to himself, "You can't talk to women. You can't tell them things that are in your heart. You can't share your feelings and your emotions with them because they will use it against you." He makes an inner vow based on his experience with his mother.

When he gets married, having forgotten that he made this earlier vow, his wife tries to get him to open up and talk. He used to share when they were courting, but now that they are married, he has become distant. What has happened is that after marriage, his wife became the "alpha" woman in his life where his mother had been the "alpha" woman before. He transferred the vow from his mother to his wife. Consequently, this man is not going to talk or share with his wife. He learned in childhood that if he told a woman something, it would be used against him. In order for their relationship to grow, that vow must be broken.

Barrenness sometimes comes upon a woman because of inner vows. One woman who was reared in a Catholic home could not conceive because of a vow she had made against her mother. She was the

80

firstborn of a large family. She grew up angry with her parents and vowing that she would never be like her mother. She was angry with her father because he continued to impregnate her mother. She was angry at her mother because she kept getting pregnant. Since her mother would be bedridden for nine months of pregnancy, she became responsible for her siblings, the household, and her father. She was also mad at the Catholic church because of their stance against birth control.

When she was nineteen, she married and left home. She had made a vow when she was a little girl that she would never be like her mother. She wanted to have children, but after she married she discovered she was unable to conceive. After going to a number of doctors, she was told there was nothing physically wrong with her or her husband to keep her from conceiving.

She sought spiritual help from me. Together, we broke the vow she had made against her mother. This included, of course, becoming pregnant. She forgave her father, her mother, and the Catholic church for their theological stance. Shortly thereafter, the young woman conceived her first child.

Vows and judgments have powerful effects. When you make a vow, God requires that you keep it!

Better is it that thou shouldst not vow, than that thou shouldst vow and not pay—Ecclesiastes 5:5.

Commonly made inner vows include: "I will never treat my children like that!" Or, "I will never be poor like my parents." Or, "I am never going to trust anyone or be vulnerable to anyone again!" Or, "My husband/wife will never treat me like that!" Beware of the words, "I will never," or, "I will always." They are often the mark of a vow.

SANDY'S STORY

With her husband by her side, Sandy told this sad and hurtful story. She was raised in a nominal Christian home. The family went to church on special occasions but the Bible, prayer, and foundational Bible truths were not taught or practiced. God was acknowledged, but true Christian faith was not lived.

As a very young girl, Sandy was sexually molested by her uncle. It continued for many years. As a result, lust was stirred up in her soul long before she needed to know about sex.

Sandy's home was largely dominated and controlled by superstitions and various kinds of occult principles. When she was about ten or eleven years old, she began to have unusual feelings about herself and experienced a strange presence in her room at night. She talked with her grandmother about this, who explained that these were "good" spirits who had come to help her. She encouraged Sandy to talk with them. Night after night, these spirits became closer to her, winning her confidence. They began to communicate with her. Their presence remained with her not only at night, but also throughout the day. She would sense their presence and receive their messages. Sandy thought this was normal.

Sandy became sexually promiscuous at an early age. Being tremendously popular in her school, she was accepted and seemed to have everything going for her. Sandy did not even realize that many things operating in her life were unnatural.

She graduated from high school and went to college, where she embraced Christianity. Later, she married a young man and started a family. She had a number of adulterous affairs along the way. Eventually she had an affair with her pastor which was devastating to her and her family.

Sandy sought my counseling and was curious why she was over-whelmed by feelings of lust and thoughts of adultery. She also wondered why she had premonitions about the future. I explained that she still had open doors to the demonic world.

Through prayer, repentance, and seeking to obey the Lord, I helped Sandy close those doors and become free from the long arm of the past. She turned from the clutches of the dark supernatural realm to the supernatural embrace of Jesus. We broke each root spirit's power over her and tore down each stronghold. She forgave those who had hurt her and broke each curse that had been passed down to her from previous generations. Sandy now walks in freedom from the dark voices and overwhelming compulsions. The dark shadows have been expelled and replaced by the spirit of the Good Shepherd, Jesus Christ.

If Satan has found legal ground in your life, either you, or someone over you, has given it to him. Otherwise, the enemy would have no authority to be there. In Sandy's case, her parents and grandparents had given place to the occult and sexual sin and thereby had opened those doors in their lives and in their bloodline. Until we prayed and closed those doors, Satan had free reign in Sandy's life, even though she had accepted the Lord Jesus and did not want to continue sinning. An ancestral curse was in operation in Sandy's life.

DOOR 5: CURSES

Have you ever felt as if you were boxing again and again with a force beyond yourself? There are invisible forces at work to determine each person's destiny. The Bible speaks about such forces, referring to them as "curses."

A curse can be compared to an extended, evil rope with one end tied to you and the other end attached to "who knows what" in the unseen past. You feel that somehow you are not in control of your own destiny. You try to get off this path of frustration but are quickly pulled back onto it. The rope holds you with a dark, unrelenting, and oppressive pressure. You feel as if you can never become who you really are. You never feel entirely free to be yourself. You sense that much of your potential lies dormant within you. You fear that it may never be completely developed. You struggle to find any sense of fulfillment and contentment in life. You may have the feeling that you are somehow different from everyone else and that you really do not fit in anywhere.

A person who is operating under a curse will often feel frustrated and disappointed. You may achieve a certain level of accomplishment and the future may look hopeful. But something always seems to happen to stop you from succeeding. Something always goes wrong—sometimes with no logical explanation. You may start over many times but reach the same unseen "glass ceiling." Time and again, things go awry. You may appear to be successful to others but never feel the satisfaction of it. You begin to recognize a pattern and wonder what dark cloud you were born under. You can neither recognize nor interpret these cycles of disappointment. Slowly you begin to silently ask, "Am I jinxed? Why does nothing ever work out right for me?"

There are two important aspects of curses:

First: The scope of their effect is almost never confined to just one individual, but more often to a larger social group or family. A curse can extend to a wide circle, such as a community or even a nation.

Second: Once a curse is released, they usually linger from generation to generation until decisive action is taken to cancel their effects.

Curses may have their origin in previous generations. There may be no explanation from your own life for some of the recurring patterns or experiences. Furthermore, the effects of a curse from an ancestor who lived hundreds of years ago may have been multiplied by your own actions. Still other curses are solely the result of your own choices.

HOW A CURSE OPERATES

The forces at work in the world fall into two categories: visible (seen) forces and invisible (unseen) forces. Forces active in the invisible sphere exert a never-ending and determined control over activities and events in the visible sphere. You cannot stop what is happening in the visible (physical) realm until you have dealt with what is happening in the invisible (spiritual) realm. The invisible realm, which houses genuine and abiding reality, contains the supernatural, spiritual power that will ultimately shape your destiny for good or evil! Both blessings and curses carry power emanating from the invisible sphere.

Surprisingly, many believers are totally unaware of the existence of curses and how they operate. This is primarily due to a Western mind-set that is hesitant to delve into the workings of the spirit realm. Others have heard of curses but consider them to be outdated Old Testament concepts. After all, they reason, didn't Christ die to set us free from the curse of the Law?

However, curses are not just Old Testament rules and regulations. They are the cause-and-effect principles that God set into motion when He made the universe. Furthermore, God's Word and His laws are unchanging.

When He came to free us from bondage, Jesus didn't come to cancel the Law. He came to fulfill it (Matthew 5:17). Since He came and conquered, we have the same power working within us through the Holy Spirit, that enables us to walk in freedom from the power of a curse! To access this power, we must repent from actions that cause curses and pray for their power to be broken. Through Christ, curses no longer have the power to hold us in bondage!

HOW CURSES ARE TRANSMITTED

Words are a major way we transmit a curse or a blessing. Words are filled with immeasurable power as they soar through the air. In fact, Scripture says that death and life are in the power of the tongue (Proverbs 18:21). With words, we bless or curse, bringing about either life or death.

Physical objects may also be vehicles to transmit the spiritual power of curses or blessings. Just as objects for blessings include holy anointing oil, the elements of the Lord's supper, and the laying on of hands, objects can be cursed and the curses transmitted knowingly or unknowingly. Occult practitioners often use physical objects to pass along curses to others. It is important to be aware that objects can carry curses.

When I was in the African jungles with a mission team, a village witch doctor insisted on giving me some dolls. I did not want to insult him, so I accepted them. Knowing the purpose of those dolls was to send a curse with me, I was not about to bring them home. As soon as we got out of range of the village, the team stopped and I tossed the dolls into a fire. We watched them burn, turning bright yellow and giving off a terrible sulfur odor.

Once I received a telephone call from a ministry friend who asked me to help cleanse the home of Christian friends who were experiencing demonic manifestations. Their children were being visited by demonic creatures in the basement, family room, and their bedrooms at night. We walked through each room of this home, praying and cleansing it of demonic spirits. When we reached the husband's office, the Lord impressed him to retrieve a handful of valuable computer chips used to illegally access cable TV programming. He began breaking them up and throwing them in the trash. His children enthusiastically joined in the spiritual house cleaning. Twelve large garbage bags full of demonic junk went to the dump. I prayed with each member of the family and broke any generational curses passed to them. Since then, there have been no further demonic visitations.

These demonic occurrences are real. Over the past twenty years, I have cleansed many homes from such objects. In some cases, the objects are not obviously demonic, because it may not be the objects themselves that are evil. It may simply be that demonic spirits are attached to them.

ANCESTRAL CURSES

Due to Adam's sin, we are all born with a natural tendency toward sin. It is our ancestral lineage, however, that determines the particular "flavor" of our desires. Ancestral curses are created by "familiar" spirits who know our family history very well. Perhaps they have been assigned to our family bloodline for hundreds or thousands of years. These "familiar" spirits transmit to you the propensities, desires, or strong tendencies from past generations. This may cause you to feel or act certain ways or have particular mannerisms. You may think these feelings are yours, because they arise frequently in your mind. However, they are actually demonic works coming through your ancestors. From birth, you will be drawn toward the sins of your forefathers, until you act-out what your forefathers practiced. It will often seem like a natural response.

It is possible to trace certain sins such as bitterness, prejudice, violence, depression, illegitimacy, prostitution, drug addiction, alcoholism, lying, stealing, physical infirmities, insanity and other sins. When giving the Ten Commandments, God said He would visit the iniquities of our forefathers to the third and fourth generation of those who hate Him (Exodus 20:5).

The Hebrew word for "iniquity" is *avon* or *avown*, which means a bent toward, a rebellion, or a perversity, a moral evil. Iniquity is more than simply an act of sin. It is a system of behavior—a way of life— that seems to have a life of its own.

One definition for the word "hate" is indifference. We do not have to be passionate, fist-shaking angry, or cursing at God to show hatred toward Him. All we have to do is to be indifferent to the voice of the Lord. Indifference is the greatest way I can hate you—by not acknowledging your personhood and acting as if you do not exist.

TRAITS OR CURSES?

Ancestral bloodline curses are so much a part of us that we often brag about them. We make excuses for them and justify them as if it were okay. We say things like, "Oh, he's just a hot-headed Irishman," or "He's just a stuck-up, stoic Englishman."

My grandfather was a full-blood Irishman. Papa had a very hot temper, an "Irish temper." So I was born with an ancestral curse of anger. As a little boy, I remember being violently angry and full of rage. When my mother would tell me no or scold me for wrong behavior, I said in defiance, "I'll just go out and turn the house over on you!" Then, I would crawl under our pier-and-beam house, put my hands against the supports, and push up on the beams until the veins popped out in my neck like little ropes.

My anger continued unabated. Like most siblings, my brother and I experienced rivalry and skirmishes. In our home the unstated rule was, "Whoever hits first, gets the spanking." My brother was seemingly better at goading me into taking the first swing than I was at coaxing him into hitting me first. Often, I got the spanking for starting the fight because I could not control my anger.

When I was about twelve, my brother and I got into a fight. Raging out of control, I reached into my pocket and took out a knife and cut him. Before I realized what I had done, the knife was jabbed deep into his arm. When it dawned on me what I had done, I tried to pull the knife out of his armbone. My parents disciplined me severely, which I certainly deserved. But later I remember falling down on my knees beside my bed. Having become a Christian the year before, I cried out to God, saying, "God, if You don't do something about my temper, I'm going to kill someone. And God, I don't want to do that." Something left me that night as I knelt beside my bed. A presence lifted off of me. From that day forward, I have never been out of control with my temper. The ancestral curse of anger was broken when I cried out to God in repentance, and through His mercy God shut that door.

Ancestral curses are one of the major ways that Satan gains legal ground into our lives. These curses can best be defined as a "strong constant propensity within us." To illustrate, a duck has a propensity toward water. He loves water. However, he does not need water to be a healthy, happy duck. If you place him in a pen and feed him, he will still be healthy. But if you place the pen near water and open the door, the duck will inevitably go in the water. He has a propensity, a drawing, a desire in that direction.

BLESSINGS AND CURSINGS

The following historical story illustrates the affects of both an ancestral curse and an ancestral blessing. Let's contrast the lives of two men who lived during the same time frame: a godless man, Max Jukes with that of a godly man, Jonathan Edwards.

Max Jukes married an unbelieving woman. From their marriage came 560 known descendants of which 300 died paupers and 150 became criminals. Seventeen were convicted murderers. One hundred were known drunkards. More than half of the women were prostitutes. The descendants of Max Jukes cost the United States government more than $1.25 million during the nineteenth century. Most of that amount was spent on their imprisonment in an effort to rehabilitate them into productive citizens.

Jonathan Edwards married a godly woman. From their union came 1,394 descendants—almost three times the number of descendants of Max Jukes. Two hundred and ninety-five of those descendants were college graduates, sixty-five became college professors, three were U.S. Senators, three were elected state governors, thirty became judges, one hundred were lawyers, one was dean of a law school, fifty-six were practicing physicians, one was dean of a medical school, seventy-five were military officers, one hundred were well-known missionaries, teachers, and authors, eighty became public officials (three of which were mayors of large cities), one was comptroller of the U.S. Treasury, and one became vice-president of the United States. None of Jonathan Edwards' descendants reportedly cost the U.S. government any money. Not one cent was spent upon the correction of the lives of these 1,394 descendants.

Common Evidences of a Curse

It would be misleading to suggest the only reason a person fails in life is due to a curse. There's a strong possibility that a curse may be operating if you recognize several of these problems occurring repeatedly in your life.

1. Insanity, personality, and emotional disturbances. Scripture lists the blessings of obedience and the curses of disobedience. When a curse is operating, depression and confusion are both prevalent.

The Lord shall smite thee with madness, and blindness, and astonishment of heart—Deuteronomy 28:28.

2. Hereditary afflictions, chronic illnesses. Heart trouble that runs in a family is a good example of a hereditary disease that emanates from a curse. When a doctor tells you that you are genetically predisposed to heart disease because your father and grandfather died with a heart attack, he is simply telling you that you have a curse operating in your life that has been passed down from your ancestors.

The Lord shall smite thee with a consumption, and with a fever, and with inflammations, and with an extreme burning— Deuteronomy 28:22.

3. Difficulties with conception, pregnancy, and other female problems. Many women are barren because a curse has been brought down upon them through an ancestral curse or from something they have done that results in a curse. Not every woman who is barren is under a curse, but many who are unable to conceive or cannot carry their baby full term have some kind of curse operating in their life.

Cursed shall be the fruit of thy body—Deuteronomy 28:18.

While ministering in a church a few years ago, I was praying over people and giving them words of knowledge that God was speaking to me. The Lord told me that a particular young woman had a curse of barrenness operating in her life. When I spoke with her and asked if she wanted to have a child, she told me that she and her husband had been trying for a long time, but she was unable to conceive. I prayed over her and broke the curse of barrenness. I told her that when I came again, I would rejoice with her over her child. When I returned 10 months later, she showed me her newborn child and we rejoiced together.

4. Divorce and division in family relationships. It is heartbreaking to look across our nation and see the family disintegrate. Even in Christian homes, marriages are being torn apart in alarming numbers. We seem unable to stop such an onslaught. Fathers and sons, and mothers and daughters, are alienated from each other, no one is willing to amend their differences and restore family relationships.

Thou shalt have sons and daughter, but thou shalt not enjoy them; for they shall go into captivity—Deuteronomy 28:41.

Tragically, divorce is now considered the norm rather than the exception in the United States.

5. Persistent financial shortage. Poverty or financial insufficiency, that is not due to lack of effort or diligence, may indicate a curse operating. If you're continuously working hard, but it seems that you are putting your money in a bag full of holes, it may be that financial curses are operating in your life.

Many believers are unaware that if they are not giving tithes and offerings, they have brought a curse upon themselves (Malachi 3:9). God does not need your money. The curse comes because you are unwilling to walk in God's way and obey Him!

However, ancestral curses may also factor into the financial hardship. For example, a man in his sixties who was about to lose his house came to me for help. Although he had previously held responsible jobs with handsome salaries, he was reduced to driving a car that belonged to someone else. As we talked, I discovered that he had made vows against his alcoholic father and had fallen into immorality several times along the way. He described this situation as a cloud overshadowing him. For ten years and a variety of unexplainable reasons, he would be fired even when he was doing an exceptional job. We prayed and broke the vows he had made against his father, he repented of his sexual immorality and other sins, and we broke the curse of poverty (Deuteronomy 28:17, 29, 47-48). Then, his life began to turn around.

6. *Being accident-prone.* If you find yourself continually in car accidents, experiencing frequent injuries, and are clumsy, it may indicate that a curse is in operation. If somebody falls down and gets hurt, it's you. You can simply walk across the room and stumble over "nothing." When you get up in the night to go to a familiar place, you run into something. Frequently you drop and break things. You are always hurting yourself in some kind of way. This is not normal. It may indicate that you are laboring under a curse (Deuteronomy 28:29).

7. *Suicide or unnatural, premature, or violent deaths.* It is not natural for suicide or untimely deaths to run through a family. The Kennedys are an example of a family that has been plagued by untimely deaths. Such numerous, untimely deaths are more than coincidence. Obviously, an ancestral curse is in operation and needs to be broken.

Other families may experience similar untimely and unnatural deaths. Perhaps a child will live to only three years old and then die, or the firstborn child will die. These are unnatural things, and are evidence of a curse in action.

CURSES MUST HAVE A PLACE TO LIGHT!

Why are some people or families bothered by curses while others are not? As Proverbs 26:2 says, "As the bird by wandering, As the swallow by flying, so the curse causeless shall not come."

A curse cannot take affect without a cause. Wherever there is a curse, you must look for the cause because it is surely there. Old Testament curses were brought on because of disobedience to God's Law.

The conditions required to enjoy the Lord's blessings are to listen to the voice of God and obey what He says.

> *If thou shalt hearken diligently unto the voice of the Lord thy God, to observe and to do all His commandments...all these blessings shall come on thee, and overtake thee, if thou shalt hearken unto the voice of the Lord thy God—Deuteronomy 28:1–2.*

In the New Testament, Jesus said that His sheep hear His voice and follow Him (John 10: 27). Blessings come to those who listen and obey. These are the unchanging requirements for living in a covenant relationship with God.

Rebellion, on the other hand, brings curses into a person's life. The consequences of rebellion are seen clearly throughout the Scriptures.

> *And then Samuel said, Hath the Lord as great delight in burnt offerings and sacrifices, as in obeying the voice of the Lord? Behold, to obey is better than sacrifice, and to hearken than the fat of rams. For rebellion is as the sin of witchcraft, and stubborn-*

ness is as iniquity and idolatry. Because thou hast rejected the word of the Lord, he hath also rejected thee from being king—1 Samuel 15:22-23.

You will open a door to demonic deception and craftiness if you step out from under authority and rebel whether you are a child under the authority of his parents, a wife under the authority of her husband, a worker under the authority of his employer, a family under the authority of the government, or a family under the authority of their pastor.

PRIMARY CAUSES OF CURSES

Here are the primary causes that bring about curses in a person's life:.

1. Disobedience and disrespect for parents. Are there areas in your parents' lives in which you have shown disrespect? Are you now having difficulty in those same areas? Perhaps they are the areas of money, authority, or relationships. Scripture admonishes us to obey and honor our parents:

Children, obey your parents in the Lord; for this is right. Honor thy father and mother, which is the first commandment with promise: That it may be well with thee, and thou mayest live long on the earth—Ephesians 6:1–3.

Often individuals focus on the promise of a long life. But this Scripture also promises that it may be well with you if you show respect to your parents. Before he was born again and entered the ministry, my pastor, Olen Griffing, was a Texas State Trooper. He shares a story that illustrates perfectly the meaning of the phrase, "that it may be well with you."

When Kent, a new State Trooper, had been on the job only two weeks, he was issued a brand-new patrol car. One day, Kent pulled out from the coffee shop onto the highway. The car's transmission fell out and scattered over the street. It took quite a bit of explaining for Kent to convince his captain that he had not been rough-housing behind the wheel of the car, and that the new car's transmission was just faulty.

Two weeks later, Kent was issued another patrol car. While riding down a West Texas road where farmers were burning cotton seed, he drove into the smoke. As he came out the other side, a car was coming head-on in his lane. To avoid an accident, Kent steered the car into a ditch and hit a telephone pole. Having wrecked another new car, Kent tried to explain what happened. After being suspended for two weeks, Kent picked up his next patrol car and started down the road. He noticed a hitchhiker and recognized him as a prison escapee. Kent picked him up and brought him back to a local courthouse. As he led the young man down to the basement of the courthouse to book him and turn him over to the proper authorities, the young man got away and ran out the door, up the stairs, and out the front door of the courthouse. Kent was in hot pursuit as the young man ran across the street to a local used-car lot. He stepped over the fourteen-inch-high railing around the car lot. Kent, however, was running at full speed and somehow caught his foot under the railing, slammed into one of the cars, broke some ribs, and wound up in the hospital. After returning to work a few weeks later, Kent went to the bank to deposit his paycheck. He parked in front of the bank, got out of his patrol car, took off his hat, and laid it in his seat. As he was walking to the bank door, he glanced up at the sky. As he did, a large hail-stone hit him between the eyes and gave him a concussion, knocking him out. Looking at Kent's life, I would say things did not go well with him!

So, if you are having a lot of difficulties in your life, it would be wise to ask the Lord if there are any ways in which you have disrespected your parents. Then, pray a prayer of repentance and ask the Lord to break any resulting curses. You may need to ask for forgiveness from your parents as well. God is serious about the things that bring curses in one's life.

2. *Acknowledging or worshipping false gods.* If you acknowledge, bow down, or worship false gods, you're bringing a curse upon yourself as well as to the third and fourth generation—your grandchildren's grandchildren!

> *I am the Lord thy God, which have brought thee out of the land of Egypt, out of the house of bondage. Thou shalt have no other gods before me—Exodus 20:1–3.*

3. *Involvement with the occult.* God hates witchcraft. There are many forms of involvement in the occult mentioned in Scripture.

> *Idolatry, witchcraft, hatred, variance, emulations, wrath, strife, seditions, heresies, envyings, revelings, and such like: of the which I tell you before as I have also told you in time past, that they which do such things shall not inherit the kingdom of God— Galatians 5:20–21.*

Witchcraft and involvement in the occult are widespread in America. It is dangerous business and a direct cause for curses. And although God's children aren't at the mercy of such curses, we are often destroyed by our lack of knowledge by any involvement in occult practices.

4. Inequity and oppression, especially aimed toward the feeble and the defenseless. God has a strong word for those who pervert justice toward the fatherless, the widow, the stranger, the helpless, and the weak. Child abuse and abortion fall within this category. It's a very strong curse that will come down upon those who take advantage of the helpless. People who take advantage of children, the simple, or the elderly will have heavy curses visited upon them.

> *Cursed be he that removeth his neighbor's landmark. And all the people shall say, Amen. Cursed be he that maketh the blind to wander out of the way. And all the people shall say, Amen. Cursed be he that perverteth the judgment of the stranger, the fatherless, and widow. And all the people shall say, Amen—Deuteronomy 27:17–19.*

5. All forbidden, aberrant, or unlawful sexual relationships. God is very explicit about sexual relationships and the penalties for violating these in His Word.

> *Cursed be he that lieth with his father's wife, because he uncovereth his father's skirt. And all the people shall say, Amen. Cursed be he that lieth with any manner of beast. And all the people shall say, Amen. Cursed be he that lieth with his sister, the daughter of his father, or the daughter of his mother. And all the people shall say, Amen. Cursed be he that lieth with his mother in law. And all shall say, Amen—Deuteronomy 27: 20–23.*

He forbids any sexual relationship outside of a husband and wife in marriage. There are actually ten different sexual sins listed in Scripture. Any violation brings grave consequences. For persons to be involved in homosexual relationships or incestuous relationships or to take advantage sexually of others is to invite a curse in their lives.

A young believer who was frustrated in her marriage shared with me that, through a series of bad decisions, she ended up in bed with another man. Coming home to an empty house while her husband was out of town, she described lying in bed that night and feeling as if flies were buzzing around her bed! In her spirit, she knew that the demonic activity around her was so stirred up as the result of her sin that the demons were rejoicing, only adding to her shame.

Not long after the incident, the doctor discovered a pre-cancerous condition resulting in surgery. After repentance and prayer, the condition was healed and her marriage restored, but the severity of the consequences of walking outside of her marriage vows remained in her mind. A tremendous amount of the pain and suffering in peoples' lives is the result of breaking God's commandment in this area. God will not be mocked. Whatever we sow, we shall reap.

6. Anti-Semitism. We need to be careful, even in jest, how we refer to the people of God. God is very serious about blessing those who bless the people of God, the Israelites, and cursing those who curse the Jewish people.

And I will bless them that bless thee, and I will curse him that curseth thee: and in thee shall all families of the earth be blessed—Genesis 12:3.

This was a blessing spoken to Abraham and the Jewish people. God's Word is the same yesterday, today, and forever.

7. Dependence upon human strength, wisdom, and goodness. People who trust in their own strength or in the strength of man are cursed.

> *Thus saith the Lord; Cursed be the man that trusteth in man, and maketh flesh his arm, and whose heart departeth from the Lord. For he shall be like the heath in the desert, and shall not see when good cometh, but shall inhabit the parched places in the wilderness, in a salt land and not inhabited—Jeremiah 17:5-6.*

Any belief in becoming righteous by our own works falls in this category. Legalism has become a strong tool in the hand of the enemy and is often used in churches against people to bring them under control and it is a curse upon them. People are told, "You have to do this or that," in order to earn favor with God." Or, "God will love you more if you do these things." The blood of Christ saves us, not what we do or don't do. Unfortunately many believers also feel strong and independent and trust their own resources. This brings a terrible curse, according to the prophet Jeremiah.

8. Stealing and lying. God is very serious about those who lie in His name, who perjure themselves, and steal. Many today are cursed from generation to generation because of the sinful actions of their ancestors.

> *Then said he unto me, This is the curse that goeth forth over the face of the whole earth: for every one that stealeth shall be cut off as on this side according to it; and every one that sweareth cut off as on that side according to it. I will bring it fourth, saith the Lord of hosts, and it shall enter into the house of the thief and into*

the house of him that sweareth falsely by my name: and it shall remain in the midst of his house, and shall consume it, with the timbers thereof the stones thereof—Zechariah 5:3-4.

CRIMES OF THE FATHER

A lengthy news article appeared in the *Dallas Morning News* entitled "Crimes of the Father." It tells parallel stories about Darrel Hill, a 57-year-old convicted killer who sits on death row in an Arkansas prison, and his son, Jeffrey Landrigan, a 37-year-old convicted killer sitting on death row in an Arizona prison. The Hill family has a long history of bootlegging, alcoholism, and violent crime.

According to the article, Darrel Hill last saw his son thirty five years ago, when he was a young junkie, locked up on a burglary charge. His son, Billy, was a baby on a jailhouse visit, nestled in his mother's arms. Soon after, Billy was adopted into a more stable, affluent family. He was given a new name, Jeffrey Landrigan, and what seemed a chance for a better life.

Hill, a third-generation criminal, continued his family's legacy of lawlessness. In 1980, after several stints in prison, he murdered a state game warden during a gas-station robbery and wound up on Arkansas' death row.

Though he grew up as Jeff Landrigan, Billy remained his father's son. A self-described misfit in the middle-class life he was given, he turned to a life of alcohol and drugs. And 1,100 miles and three decades removed, he sits on Arizona's death row, a two-time killer just like the father he never knew. Jeff never knew his father and yet he followed in his father's and his ancestors' footsteps. A prisoner in jail with Jeff in Arizona had previously been in jail in Arkansas and recognized the similarities between the two men. This was how Jeff Landrigan learned the identity of his birth father.

Jeff's birth mother said, "They look alike, talk alike, sound alike, and think alike. It's mind-blowing." Yet, these two men have never met face-to-face. Reading in the article the details of their separate lives is like comparing carbon copies. The article also speaks of the possibility of some kind of "killing gene" which is inherited. This is truly a classic example of ancestral sins being visited upon the third and fourth generations (Source: *Dallas Morning News*, October 20, 1997).

9. Withholding of tithes and offerings. When you take material resources which belong to God and withhold them from Him, you are bringing a curse upon yourself.

> *Will a man rob God? Yet ye have robbed me. But ye say, Wherein have we robbed thee? In tithes and offerings. Ye are cursed with a curse: for ye have robbed me, even this whole nation—Malachi 3:8–9.*

10. Words spoken by those in authority. Those in authority include fathers, mothers, husbands, wives, teachers, pastors, and priests—anyone who has a position of authority over us. Words spoken by a father over his children are the most powerful words in the universe besides God's own words. A father's piercing words, such as, "You're dumb, you're stupid, you're crazy," have cursed his children to grow up and fulfill the exact words that were spoken.

Women will tell me often in ministry sessions that as young girls they lived immorally because their fathers repeatedly called them whores, and other words of this nature. They believed the words, and began to live out what their fathers accused them of being.

*With whomsoever thou findest thy gods, let him not live: before
our brethren discern thou what is thine with me, and take it to
thee. For Jacob knew not that Rachel had stolen them—Genesis
31:32.*

Jacob did not know that Rachel had taken the gods from her
father, Laban, when the family left Laban's land. Not long after, Rachel
died in childbirth. Unknowingly, Jacob had spoken a death curse over
his wife.

11. Negative idle words pronounced by anyone against themselves.
Many people have brought curses upon themselves by constantly saying, "I can't. I can't do this. I can't do that. I can't do something else."
They put themselves down, constantly speaking negatively about
themselves. They don't realize they are binding themselves by their
own words.

*But I say unto you, that every idle word that men shall speak, they
shall give account thereof in the day of judgment. For by thy words
thou shalt be justified, and by thy words thou shalt be condemned—Matthew 12:36–37.*

A young single mother was constantly frustrated by the quality
and character of the men coming in and out of her life. She was beginning to think of herself as a "jerk-magnet" and couldn't understand
why so many immoral, lying men were attracted to her. Speaking to a
godly friend about it one night after dinner, he helped her to see the
problem. She'd grown up with a father of great character, who,
although he had many wonderful qualities, wasn't a Christian. And,
after going to a private Christian college and seeing the way many

Christian young men behaved, she at many times in her life had said these words: "I will never marry a Christian man." She broke the curse of her idle words and within six months, a wonderful Christian man came into her life, lovingly embracing her and her children.

Psychology terms this a "self-fulfilling prophecy." Whatever you believe about yourself, you will become. It's a vicious circle; whatever you perceive about yourself, you will speak. Whatever you speak, you will believe. Whatever you believe, you speak, and so on. Watch your words!

12. Oaths or covenants taken for admission to secret societies and ungodly organizations.

Thou shalt make no covenant with them, nor with their gods—Exodus 23:32.

Many people make covenants and pledges to organizations and brotherhoods that require them to take blood oaths and make oaths concerning what will happen to them. An example is the oath taken in Freemasonry. To make an oath to any kind of fraternal organization that requires you to sign your name in blood, stating that your heart may be cut out or that you may be killed if you divulge its secrets, is ungodly. Freemasonry is a false religion serving a false god and has strong generational curses associated with it. Many physical infirmities can be traced to the roots of such oaths taken, involving desecration of various bodily organs.

13. Curses that are pronounced by witches, warlocks, witchdoctors, or other occultists. Curses spoken upon people by the enemy or servants of the enemy can be binding and debilitating (Ezekiel

13:17–23). In Africa, many witchdoctors and witches hold people in fear because the people know the power of these spoken curses. Often a curse of barrenness will make a woman unable to conceive, or a curse spoken on a man will prevent him from fathering children. While traveling in Africa, I heard of witches putting a curse on chicken bones. The person who ate the chicken would be dead by the next morning.

I talked with a woman whose mother was a witch. Because of various conflicts in the relationship, the mother declared to the daughter, "You will never buy property and live peacefully." Three times the daughter bought property, but each time numerous "things" began to happen; the neighbors were extremely hostile with no reason; items would be missing from the house or strange objects would appear in the house. Each time the property was sold because of such harassment.

A witch who was converted several years ago shared with me that covens on a regular basis send out curses of division, divorce, contention, immorality, etc. against pastors, ministers, and their children. With the tremendous rise in witchcraft in recent years, Christians have seen a great increase in these types of curses. We may not even know that it is operating, but those who are especially effective in the Kingdom of God may find themselves feeling that the spiritual atmosphere around them has changed and that "something is not right." In several cases, the root has been a witchcraft curse.

These witchcraft curses are very real and powerful. Do not become involved in any way with anything occultic, or give the enemy a place for such a curse to light. Through the weapons provided for us by Jesus, we can be protected and these witchcraft curses can be broken.

14. Carnal talk directed against others. Have you ever heard someone say, "Oh, we need to pray for Lance and Kim. They are getting a divorce because he's been having an affair with Laura." That isn't showing genuine concern; it's gossiping!

> *But if ye have bitter envying and strife in your hearts, glory not, and lie not against the truth. This wisdom descendeth not from above, but is earthly, sensual, devilism. For where envying and strife is, there is confusion and every evil work—James 3:14–15.*

15. *Manipulating prayers that accuse or seek to control others.* This is praying what you want instead of God's will. It is seeking to manipulate and control others through the spiritual means of prayer. Accusation can also be a key component of this type of prayer.

> *He that turneth away his ear from hearing the law, even his prayer shall be abomination—Proverbs 28:9.*

CONCLUSION

Through the five open doors mentioned in this chapter, Satan has the legal right to walk into your life, torment you, bring you into bondages of all kinds, and unleash tremendous frustration in you. As a result you may find you are unable to be what God has called you to be or to do what God has called you to do. That's what Satan wants! To steal your destiny! But you have the authority in the name of Jesus to stop him in his tracks. Do it!

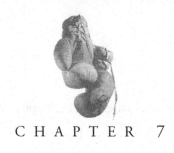

CHAPTER 7

HOLDING

Have you wondered why you cannot be freed from the patterns that keep recurring in your life? You're in the ring and Satan's "holding," but the referee won't stop him? Or does it seem as if you're on a permanent merry-go-round? You find yourself falling into the same sin again and again, each time promising God that this time will be the last. Secretly you hope He will bail you out and deliver you from the consequences! But in a few weeks, a few days, a few hours, a few moments, you find yourself riding around again. This merry-go-round of failure is called a stronghold.

Through one or more of the five open doors, Satan has access into your life and the legal right to be there anytime he wishes. He then begins a "holding" pattern in your life, systematically setting up strongholds that will keep you bound in place.

A stronghold is a place of fortification, a system of thinking contrary to the Word of God. Francis Frangipane defines a stronghold as a "house of lies." It's a place where demonic spirits hide, live, and work undercover.

Ann's Story

Ann, a sixty-year-old successful businesswoman, came to me for ministry. Her husband, also a professional, had died of a heart attack a few years earlier. Ann had deep feelings of inferiority and a poor self-image. She was overweight because she constantly ate to comfort herself. Ann's father was a police officer. He was highly respected and a man of integrity. Her mother was also a professional woman.

She began to tell me the story of her childhood. Her father wanted a son, and he verbally stated throughout her mother's pregnancy that the baby was going to be a son who would grow up to be a policeman like him. He spoke all of these expectations over this baby in the womb. Then came forth this beautiful little girl. Ann's father loved her, cared for her, and provided for her; but he was disappointed that she was not a boy. Ann received the message in the womb and out of the womb that her father wanted her to be a boy, but God made her a girl. She grew up believing she was the wrong sex. So she became a "tomboy." She was never interested in dolls and lace and the things girls do, nor in keeping house or those types of things. She did all sorts of "boy" things like climbing trees and picking up bugs and putting them in her pockets.

Ann had severe feelings of inferiority, feeling in her own heart she should have been a man, believing she had a man's mentality but that she was trapped in a woman's body. As she grew up, this caused her to have feelings of attraction toward the same sex. She could never shake this desire to be a man. It haunted her and caused her to feel inferior and inadequate in her marriage and as a mother. When her husband died, it caused her to continue to feel she could never reach the destiny God had for her.

I ministered to her and broke the lies of the enemy off her, those strongholds of rejection and inferiority. She had always hated womens' clothes that were dainty and feminine, and so she always wore rougher denim and mannish clothes. We broke these curses spoken over her by her father's words in the womb and even after she was born. Suddenly, the very way that she carried her body and even the way she walked became more feminine.

She is now grateful that God made her to be a woman and not a man. She no longer dresses in masculine clothes. Her feelings of deep inferiority are gone, and today she is fifty pounds lighter than she was when I led her through ministry. She no longer has to struggle to keep her weight off. She has received from the Lord all that He has for her. She is walking in her destiny as the woman of God she was created to be.

SATAN'S LIES

Satan doesn't just walk into your life and announce he's going to set up a stronghold. He begins to gradually feed lies into your mind which will eventually destroy you. He exalts arguments and vain imaginations (impossible fantasies) as barriers against the knowledge of God. He knows that if we believe the truth, then his power over us is finished.

In the case study at the beginning of this chapter, Satan lied to Ann and tried to convince her she was meant to be a man. She believed his lie, and as strongholds of rejection and inferiority were solidified, her entire life was affected. She was unable to overcome the battle in her mind until the strongholds were torn down and broken—by the power of Jesus Christ. Once she was able to believe the truth, Ann became the graceful woman God created her to be.

KNOWING THE TRUTH

You may know the truth in your mind but still live out a lie in your daily experience, because knowing something in your mind doesn't necessarily enable you to live it. "Knowing the truth" is not mental assent to some theological doctrine but rather intimacy with the Truth—Jesus Christ. Truth becomes "at home" in you; it becomes such a part of your belief system that you respond and react accordingly. Therefore, if you know the Truth of God, you will be free from lies binding you. Even though Satan is an expert at lies, deceptions, and fears, knowing the Truth will allow you to walk victoriously.

And ye shall know the truth, and the truth shall make you free—John 8:32.

Often it's easier to believe the lie than the truth, because we've been trained in the "lie" as children. Our culture propagates and supports the "lie." For instance, how were you and I taught to become rich? By getting all that we can, keeping every bit of it, and not letting anyone else have any of it! Therefore, greed and selfishness are the world's way to riches. Contrary to this lie, Jesus said that in order to be rich, you must give it away.

Jesus told the rich young ruler:

If thou wilt be perfect, go and sell that thou hast, and give to the poor, and thou shalt have treasure in heaven; and come and follow me—Matthew 19:21.

The young ruler turned and walked away because he couldn't bring himself to give up his earthly riches.

The world's system says in order to be first, you must get ahead of everyone else. You must get there before they get there, and maintain your position by whatever means necessary. Yet Jesus said if you want to be first, then choose to be last.

The majority of us don't accept this truth in our daily lives. We may acknowledge it as truth, but one quick glance at society tells all. Most of us have learned to say the right words of doctrine, but our attitudes and actions reveal what we really believe about God. As my friend Peter Lord says, "We practice daily all that we believe and all else is religious talk."

Another lie from the world is that to "find yourself" you must search inside until you discover who your "self" is. But Truth says that if you want to "find yourself," you must give your life away to others! The world says we must seek self-fulfillment and our own happiness at all costs, ignoring the needs of others. But Truth says that to really live, you must first die to yourself. You will never find your life following the lie. And the thought patterns built up around even one lie can become a whole system of deception through which Satan can practice his "holding" for a very long time.

THE PROGRESSION OF A STRONGHOLD

Strongholds develop progressively, first beginning with the willingness to cooperate, or ignorantly cooperating, with some activity from the demonic world. For example, if I choose to become involved in some kind of illicit sexual encounter and I experience pleasure, out of that experience comes an emotion. From that emotion, thoughts are created. I think about what I've done, which creates an emotion again, which creates more thoughts. And then if I'm not careful, I'll find myself committing that action again because I have been stimulated by thoughts and emotions! As I continue to act in that same manner, I'm forming a habit in my life. As a habit is formed, a lifestyle or way of life is formed. And when a way of life is formed, a fully formed stronghold is established.

I've now built a system of lies to support my actions and cover my guilt. Satan has captured my will by my cooperating with him, either knowingly or unknowingly, in this area of my life. His next step is to begin to build supporting strongholds—such as lying to cover my immorality.

Other early experiences—such as molestation—also lead to strongholds, even though we were victimized and not responsible for the sin perpetrated against us. It's not the experience itself that causes a stronghold to develop, but what we believe about the experience, about God, and about ourselves as a result of the experience. Any traumatic experience, the making of vows, or not forgiving someone who has hurt us will multiply the strongholds, putting us in prison.

The following story illustrates the progression of a stronghold and the difficulty of spending "life in prison."

DEBBIE'S STORY

Debbie writes how her life was ruled by a strange darkness: From as far back as I can remember, I always had an uncomfortable sense of being different from everyone else. I didn't know why, but it's how I felt.

I didn't get the idea from my extended family. To them, I was adorable, outstanding, and brilliant. My mother's parents treated me as a special treasure. My aunt and uncle always bought me fun and wonderful things. I was their first niece and they showed me off with great pride. My father's older brother, having no children of his own, cherished me like a royal jewel. He showered me with expensive toys, gifts, clothes, and jewelry. He chauffeured his French wife and me to fabulous places and grand openings of shows, restaurants, and hotels, always in his ever-new expensive shiny cars.

It would have all been the best of lives except for one serious problem—my father detested me. I was an extremely intelligent child, but I never could figure out why my father hated me. He wouldn't hold me, touch me, or say anything kind. If I tried to climb into his lap, desperate for his affection, he would roughly shove me away saying, 'Get out of here, kid. You bother me.'

My mother tried everything to bring him to love me. She taught me songs, orchestrated dance routines and skits. Although she and I would perform flawlessly, my father would rarely look up from his newspaper. If he did, he would make a cruel, derogatory remark about me. Throughout life, if I ever excelled at anything, he degraded me for it.

My mother seemed to love me a lot. She took good care of me, fed me, and did all the things a mother should do. Deep down inside, though, I had a dreadful fear of her and knew I'd better be careful.

Between the two of them, I lived in a constant state of dread. Many of my feelings were centered around being abandoned or kidnapped—especially during the night when I was in bed.

When I was only three-and-a-half years old, I was so traumatized and confused that I actually tried to commit suicide! Fully conscious of what I was doing, I ate bug-poison tablets but nothing happened. My abysmal self-hatred and condemnation continued. My only solace in life was when I was with my mother's parents. My wonderful, wealthy uncle rarely came to town anymore, and my other relatives lived in a different state. But my grandparents still treated me like I was a special gift.

My grandfather and I were especially close. He was my "Papa" who loved me more than anyone. We played games and danced. He cared for me dearly. Then, he suddenly died. I grieved for him and for my life without him.

During that same year, I went to the movies with friends. With no announcement, the western movie that was supposed to be showing had been changed to a 3-D horror movie called *House of Wax*. With no adult supervision, I sat in complete innocence watching the movie. The victim was a woman, kidnapped from her bed during the night (my worst fear) by a man whose face had been destroyed by fire. That movie connected with something deep within me and I was never the same again.

For the next two years I couldn't sleep at night for fear of being kidnapped. A horrifying, recurrent nightmare began and continued all of my life. I was so nervous and terrified that I began having frequent illnesses.

My parents divorced when I was eight. By then, I had a little sister whom my father loved dearly. My sister and I lived with my mother, moving from place to place, which made it hard to have friends. It seemed as if an invisible someone or something was orchestrating my life to keep me isolated and alone.

My mother worked, did her best to pay bills, and spent the rest of her time trying to find her identity with strange people. My mother had an innate ability to attract morally depraved men, and I was extremely frightened of them. By age eleven, I couldn't tolerate living with her anymore and begged and pleaded until I was allowed to live with my father and his new wife. However, they were very strict with me and demonstrated no patience or kindness toward helping me to understand their high demands. I remember being reduced to tears daily.

Inevitably, I ended up back with my mother who by this time had been married two more times. My mother's third husband was sadistically cruel and beat me severely on a regular basis. He always threatened to kill me during the night; therefore, I slept with a large kitchen knife under my pillow.

Conditions finally became so adverse that at age twelve I decided to check out. One day while everyone was gone, I ate an entire bottle of aspirin. Nothing happened! Nobody ever even knew what I had attempted. And once again, I went back to live with my father.

I couldn't stand the neglect, stress, and abuse anymore, so in my early teens I left home and struck out on my own. I went to another state, knowing that I could do a better job of raising myself. I figured I had all the basics covered; I could read, write, file, type, and ward off maniacs and perverts.

During this time I began studying psychology in an effort to psychoanalyze myself. I read books, tried all kinds of therapy on myself, went to seminars, always searching for that elusive thing other people seemed to possess called normalcy.

God was never discussed in the households in which I grew up except for "cutesy" bedtime prayers before I was three years old. As an adult, the Lord Jesus Christ, in His great love and mercy, allowed me a phenomenal salvation experience in which He appeared to me. It was instant salvation as I fell on my face in absolute recognition, fear, and reverence. I immediately began searching for a church to attend. I drifted in and out of various denominations.

Having no discipleship and not even understanding what the Bible really meant or even how to read it effectively, I didn't know how to walk closely with the Lord. In my efforts to find a deeper relationship with Christ, I became absorbed with the New Age and the occult with all the mind-binding illusions, powerful false beliefs, and demonic inroads. I became deeply involved honestly believing I was following Jesus!

I moved around quite a bit. In Chicago, still in my teens, I was 'discovered' as a singer and even signed a contract that could have taken me to great acclaim, but fear drove me away. Being under age, I broke the contract. Two years later I became a model in New York and had the opportunity to sign up with the top agency in the country. I might have become world-famous but again fear intervened, and I quickly ran away from that too. Deep inner fear drove me like a harsh master. I had other opportunities to become wildly successful and famous but that "something" deep within always veered me away. Then five years later, I had a most unusual experience.

While living on the West Coast, I returned to New York to visit some friends. One afternoon I was sitting alone in the apartment doing my Eastern meditation when suddenly, I felt as if I melted down through the floor into an underworld. I found myself in a chasm filled with a total absence of light—pitch-black oblivion. In front of me was a golden throne and sitting on the throne was some sort of being, shrouded in the same darkness as was behind the throne.

Suddenly a velvety black, consuming voice came from the darkness sitting on the throne. It declared authoritatively that I could have great fame and fortune, if I would just worship him. In a split-second, the blackness and evil force became acutely real and I knew who was speaking. This was no joke but a bona fide, genuine encounter with Satan. Suddenly without thinking, there arose from the depth of my being a great swelling. I heard my own voice bellow, "Jesus Christ is my Lord and Savior!" I was instantly back in the apartment, badly shaken.

Finally, the Lord led me to a church and I began separating the lies from the half-truths I had been taught. I became a true and everlasting disciple of Jesus Christ. Revival broke out in our church and I was there almost every night for two months. The more I sought and obeyed Him, the more He moved in my life. Even though I was now a strong Christian, I still felt I hadn't attained normalcy. I wasn't completely free from the fear and I still felt like something was trying to take over my mind. It was terrifying. How could this happen to a born-again, on fire, Holy Ghost anointed Christian?

I sought help from secular psychologists. They helped to a minimal extent, but they didn't believe that demons existed. The strangest most bizarre things would take place while I would be working with one of these counselors. It was frightening.

Next I tried to derive help from Christian pastors only to be told, 'Christians can't have demons.' One ministry finally humored me by praying for me to prove that there was nothing there. What a shock they had when a hideous demon manifested. They had no idea how to handle the situation and that horrid devil attacked them bodily before leaving. What a glorious deliverance I had though! I spent the next three days praising, worshipping, and thanking the Lord. On the third day that foul spirit came right back to me even though I tried to resist.

My life really got bad as I was going in and out of terror, often being tormented by demons. I avoided people except to attend church. I sought every resource for information to find someone who knew the power of God for true deliverance and was not a quack. At last, somebody recommended Dr. Malone. By the time of my appointment, I felt I'd crossed six mighty mountain ranges, swam an ocean, and crossed the Sahara desert barefoot with a thimble of water!"

Debbie and I discussed everything in great depth. We found the open doors to the demonic, and commanded the evil to leave her. With the demonic suffocation gone, the "underbrush was cleared" and she could begin to deal with the problems built up over all the years.

Through several other sessions, God began restoring, repairing, and making Debbie whole.

"Suddenly the oppression was gone and I was free," said Debbie. It was like having a bath from the inside out. Darkness left and the Holy Spirit bathed me in glorious light within and without. My mind was amazingly clear. The trouble in my life wasn't because of mental problems or even strange personality traits, but demons from hell operating through ancestral sin and curses generationally passed down to me. What a miserable inheritance!"

The purpose of the strongholds in Debbie's life was to keep her from knowing God as He really is—loving, good, faithful, powerful, and gracious! Lies and deception have at their root a wrong view of God Himself.

THE PURPOSE OF STRONGHOLDS

As he did in Debbie's life, Satan exalts lies in our lives too. He sets up strong places of fortification and rules us by the lies he gets us to believe! He never uses truth, but he very skillfully uses facts, circumstances, events, and credible people to deceive and delude us.

To illustrate, most of us have known of at least one friend who has ended up in an extramarital affair. How did this affair begin? Satan saw an open door and decided to attack. The deceitful lies planted were tiny at first, probably beginning at the start of the marriage. "I don't really like that thing about her, but I love her so I can live with it." And the lie gradually built to "I've always known I didn't like that thing about her, I just couldn't admit it to myself." Until, upon meeting someone else, it becomes, "I knew she wasn't my soul-mate, she had that thing about her I didn't like. I have always known, I just could not admit it."

We stand by and watch as the little deception becomes a marriage-breaking stronghold, often making the person we thought we knew so well look absolutely foolish.

After twelve years of what seemed to be a great marriage, a beautiful young woman's husband walked out and filed for divorce. After finding out adultery was involved, this young woman pleaded, "Please try to explain to me why this happened. What did this woman have that I don't have? I really need to know." And her intelligent, successful husband said, "We just have more in common. We both like red licorice and the ends of the loaf of bread."

Strongholds work through our flesh or the "old man." Whenever I give into the flesh by believing Satan's lies, the enemy is able to come into my mind and build mental strongholds in my life. Thus, Satan can capture my will to do whatever he desires. But as believers, we are taught to walk in the Spirit:

> *Walk in the Spirit, and ye shall not fulfill the lust of the flesh. For the flesh lusteth against the Spirit, and the Spirit against the flesh: and these are contrary the one to the other: so that ye cannot do the things that ye would. But if ye be led of the Spirit, ye are not under the law...If we live in the Spirit, let us also walk in the Spirit—Galatians 5:16–18, 25.*

It's the power of the Holy Spirit alone that can overcome the strength of the flesh. If I walk in the Spirit, I will not fulfill the lust of the flesh. I will stand against the temptation to believe Satan's ridiculous lies!

As believers, we are instructed to pull down every high thing that exalts itself against the knowledge of God, to renew our minds and to bring every thought into captivity.

For though we walk in the flesh, we do not war after the flesh. For the weapons of our warfare are not carnal, but mighty through God to the pulling down of strongholds. Casting down imaginations and every high thing that exalteth itself against the knowledge of God, and bringing into captivity every thought to the obedience of Christ—2 Corinthians 10:3–6.

Truth is unchanging. It's the same yesterday, today, and forever. To stand against Satan's lies, we must live in the truth—eat it, drink it, breathe it, sleep it. It must abide in us. And that truth is Jesus.

C H A P T E R 8

THE FOURTEEN ROOT SPIRITS

One day a mother telephoned me desperate for help with her seven-year-old son. The young boy was tormented by seizures and had severe allergies. She pleaded with me to pray for her son. So, I met with each of the parents, leading them through deliverance and inner healing. Then, I agreed to see their son. When ministering to a child, it is necessary to be sure the parents are walking in freedom, because they are in authority over the child. Also, it is important to note that autism is not always caused by spiritual strongholds, although often that is the case.

As I talked with the parents about ancestral curses, ancestral sins, and strongholds, it became very evident that Tommy had a stronghold caused by a deaf-and-dumb spirit that had been handed down from one generation to the next. It was an ancestral curse. This deaf-and-dumb spirit connected with the spirit of fear and the spirit of bondage had brought Tommy to the place where he was. The father and mother, I learned, had both been tormented with a deaf-and-dumb spirit but in a different way than their son was tormented.

As the parents prepared Tommy to come and see me, he was peaceful and agreeable. On the drive to my office that morning, he was happy and did not have any seizures. When the car turned into our driveway, Tommy began to have one seizure after another. By the time they entered my office, Tommy was extremely nervous, angry, and uncooperative.

When Tommy was born, the doctor told his parents they should put him in an institution because he would never walk, talk, or live a normal life. Because the parents believed God could and would set their child free, they refused to put Tommy away. The first six years of his life, Tommy nearly died again and again because he was allergic to almost all foods. He was literally starving because he could not eat enough food to keep him alive.

Tommy came into my office with his eyes flashing, extremely nervous, and very agitated. His eyes were dark and had an empty look in them. His countenance was closed and drawn. He had the look of someone in whom the "lights are on" but no one is home.

I began leading his parents in a prayer of repentance for the sins of their ancestors. We made a verbal confession of who they were in Christ. After this, I anointed Tommy with oil and began to break the curses and strongholds off this seven-year-old boy's life. When I laid hands on him, he began to wiggle and squirm. As I continued to pray, the demons began to cry out and make different kinds of noises. When I addressed the deaf-and-dumb spirit, Tommy's head swung around and his eyes enlarged with a very resistant look. I continued to pray until he fell into his mother's arms, relaxed and relieved. When the spirits were gone, Tommy was free.

When the ministry time was over, Tommy was smiling. He lifted his head and talked to us. His countenance had changed remarkably. His face was even shaped differently than when he came into my office! I asked Tommy how he was feeling. He said, "Good, good, good." This seven-year-old boy could say words he had never been able to say and was no longer having seizures.

Thank God, Jesus broke the power of a deaf-and-dumb spirit in Tommy's life, and he was set free. I talked with his parents a few weeks later. He was gaining weight, eating foods he had not eaten before, and was no longer having seizures.

There are at least fourteen sins listed in Scripture that are specifically identified as "spirits." These fourteen root spirits weave themselves in and out of the five legal doors, creating a root-and-fruit system and often producing a proliferation of problems in people's lives. It should come as no surprise that the kingdom of darkness works from a root-and-fruit system in much the same way as the Kingdom of Light, because Satan counterfeits everything God does!

The works of the flesh (kingdom of darkness) and the fruit of the Spirit (Kingdom of Light) are contrasted in this passage from Galatians:

Now the works of the flesh are manifest, which are these: adultery, fornication, uncleanness, lasciviousness, idolatry, witchcraft, hatred, variance, emulations, wrath, strife, seditions, heresies, envyings, murders, drunkenness, revelings, and such like; of the which I tell you before, as I have also told you in time past, that they which do such things shall not inherit the kingdom of God. But the fruit of the Spirit is love, joy, peace, longsuffering, gentleness, goodness, faith, meekness, temperance: against such there is no law. And they that are Christ's have crucified the flesh with the affections and lusts—Galatians 5:19–24.

When we are "rooted and grounded" in Jesus, the Holy Spirit produces His wonderful fruit of godly character within us, whereas the evil fruit of the kingdom of darkness is produced by an evil root system.

To illustrate, pretend you have a large apple tree in your front yard. You look out one morning and see red apples on it. You've recently decided that you hate red apples, and you'll have nothing more to do with them. You get a sack and pick all the red apples off the tree and throw them in the trash! You say to yourself, "I am now through with this red-apple thing."

But, of course, you are only through with it for a season! Because you only picked the fruit, the root in the ground next season will send up more red apples! When apple season comes again, there they are as big and red as ever. Now you're really determined! Again, you pick all the apples and throw them in the trash. Then you saw off all the limbs of the tree and throw them in the trash, also! Once again you say to yourself, "Now I am really through with this red-apple thing."

But once again, next season, you're in an even worse dilemma. The root in the ground has gone deeper and become larger because you practiced the principle of pruning.

Every branch in me that beareth not fruit he taketh away: and every branch that beareth fruit, he purgeth, that it may bring forth more fruit—John 15:2.

This year you find more red apples and larger red apples on your tree than you have ever had before! You go out with your sack and so on.

I've heard from many that they've "tried" deliverance, but it didn't work for them. Could it be that someone only picked the fruit off the tree and didn't cut the root? Unless you pull down the strongholds and cut the roots of these fourteen spirits, you will constantly have to deal with the fruit of these specific roots again at certain times in your life!

Through my experiences with the ministry of deliverance, I have seen Satan use the fourteen root spirits—each root spirit characteristically producing certain fruit—to set up strongholds in peoples' lives. Although the following list is not exhaustive, it will give you an understanding of how and where these root spirits may be operating in your life.

1. SPIRIT OF INFIRMITY

And behold there was a woman which had a spirit of infirmity eighteen years, and was bowed together and could in no wise lift up herself—Luke 13:11.

- lingering disorders of the body
- weakness or feebleness
- cancer
- female problems
- fungus
- fevers
- allergies
- sinus problems
- high blood pressure
- attacks on femininity
- attacks on masculinity
- arthritis
- heart disease
- diabetes

2. SPIRIT OF FEAR

For God hath not given us the spirit of fear; but of power, and of love, and of a sound mind—2 Timothy 1:7.

- fright
- torment
- nightmares
- fear of death
- faithlessness
- timidity
- shyness
- inferiority
- inadequacy
- rejection
- worry
- anxiety
- critical spirit
- tensions
- stress (heart attacks)
- fear of failure
- performance
- fear of man (what others think of you)
- fear of poverty
- migraine headaches
- schizophrenia
- paranoia
- insanity
- lack of trust
- phobias (fears of dark, height, water, closed-in places, etc.)
- fear/sense of abandonment
- fear of pain
- fear of men (because of abuse)
- fear of women
- fear of authority

3. SPIRIT OF DIVINATION

And it came to pass, as we went to prayer, that a certain damsel possessed with a spirit of divination met us, which brought her masters much gain by soothsaying. The same followed Paul and us, and cried, saying, These men are servants of the most high God, which shew unto us the way of salvation. And this she did for many days. But Paul, being grieved, turned and said to the spirit, I command thee in the name of Jesus Christ to come out of her. And he came out the same hour—Acts 16:16–18.

- independence
- mediums
- horoscopes
- rebellion
- stubbornness
- Satanism (worship of Satan)
- mutterer (one who talks with a familiar spirit as if talking to himself)
- diviners (witches)
- astrology
- Ouija boards
- seances
- white witchcraft
- channeling
- Tarot cards
- palm readers
- games (Masters of the Universe, Dungeons and Dragons, Magic 8 Ball, Pokémon, etc.)
- crystal balls
- mysticism
- transcendental meditation
- drugs
- unscriptural attempts at deliverance (those that do not line up with the Word)
- fortune-tellers
- Freemasonry or secret organizations
- Eastern religions

4. SPIRIT OF WHOREDOMS

My people ask counsel at their stocks, and their staff declareth unto them, for the spirit of whoredoms has caused them to err, and they have gone a whoring from under their God—Hosea 4:12.

- adultery
- molestation
- rape
- incest
- lust
- pornography
- masturbation
- harlotry

- seduction
- exhibition of the body
- peeping toms
- multi-partner sex orgies
- all sexual sins
- bestiality
- idolatry

- love of money
- love of the world
- love of social standing
- anything worshipped or trusted in for security
- lust for position
- placing anyone or anything before God

5. SPIRIT OF BONDAGE

For ye have not received the spirit of bondage again to fear; but ye have received the Spirit of adoption, whereby we cry, Abba, Father—Romans 8:15.

- cigarettes
- alcohol
- drugs
- bulimia
- anorexia
- soul ties (under the power and dominion of another)
- superiority (addicted to self)
- addicted to a specific sin

- addicted to another person (co-dependency)
- workaholism
- pornography
- sex
- computers
- video games
- food
- television

128

6. SPIRIT OF HAUGHTINESS

Pride goeth before destruction, and an haughty spirit before a fall.
Better it is to be of an humble spirit with the lowly, than to divide
the spoil with the proud—Proverbs 16:18–19.

- pride
- scorn
- mockery
- judgment
- rudeness
- lofty looks
- bragging
- stubbornness
- egotism
- prejudice
- self-righteousness or holier-than-thou attitude
- vanity (exalted feelings about self)
- arrogance
- dictatorial
- controlling
- overbearing
- domineering
- superiority
- gossip
- contention
- constant criticism
- independence

7. SPIRIT OF PERVERSENESS

The Lord hath mingled a perverse spirit in the midst thereof; and
they have caused Egypt to err in every work thereof, as a drunk-
en man staggereth in his vomit—Isaiah 19:14.

- homosexuality
- multi-partner sex orgies
- sadomasochism
- unreasonableness
- error (especially in religious areas)
- abnormal crankiness

- all sexual deviations
- false teachers
- self-lovers
- one who twists the Word of God to Satan's advantage
- stubbornness
- polygamy
- involvement with false doctrine and/or occult

8. SPIRIT OF ANTICHRIST

And every spirit that confesseth not that Jesus Christ is come in the flesh is not of God: and this is that spirit of the antichrist, whereof ye have heard that is should come, and even now already is it in the world—1 John 4:3.

- attempts to take the place of Christ
- opposes the Bible
- opposes Christ's deity, doctrine, victory, and humanity (cults)
- harasses the saints
- persecutes the saints
- martyrs the saints
- suppresses ministries and causes church splits
- blasphemes the gifts of the Holy Spirit, attributing them to Satan
- rationalizes the Word of God
- explains away all the power of God in the life of the saint (no miracles)
- Judaism
- gives up on Christianity
- atheism

9. SPIRIT OF DEAF AND DUMBNESS

When Jesus saw that the people came running together, he rebuked the foul spirit, saying unto him, "Thou dumb and deaf spirit, I charge thee, come out of him, and enter no more into him. And the spirit cried, and rent him sore, and came out of him: And he was as one dead; insomuch that many said, He is dead. But Jesus took him by the hand, and lifted him up: and he arose—Mark 9:25–27.

- convulsions
- seizures
- stupor
- grinding of the teeth
- epilepsy
- suicide attempts and tendencies
- madness
- insanity
- schizophrenia
- diseases of the eyes and ears
- accidents with water (drowning) and burning
- inappropriate excessive crying
- deafness
- autism (in certain instances)

10. SPIRIT OF HEAVINESS

To appoint unto them to console all who mourn in Zion, to give unto them beauty for ashes, the oil of joy for mourning, the garment of praise for the spirit of heaviness; that they might be called trees of righteousness, the planting of the Lord, that he might be glorified—Isaiah 61:3.

- depression
- abnormal mourning
- continual sorrow
- abnormal grief
- continual sadness
- despair
- hopelessness
- loneliness
- shame
- defilement

- discouragement
- rejection
- self-pity
- whining
- gloominess

- wounded spirit
- unjustified guilt
- brokenheartedness
- humiliation

11. SPIRIT OF LYING

Now therefore, behold, the Lord has put a lying spirit in the mouth of thy prophets, and the Lord hath spoken evil against thee—2 Chronicles 18:22.

- lies
- strong delusions
- deception
- flattery
- exaggeration
- excessive talking
- profanity
- hypocrisy
- emotionalism
- religious spirit (legalism)
- condemnation
- lies about God
- vain imaginations

- daydreaming
- performance
- financial problems (if you are tithing)
- poor self image
- "You are ugly!"
- "You are worthless!"
- "Stupid!"
- "You will never get married!"
- "No one wants you!"
- "You're trash!"
- "You will never change!"

12. SPIRIT OF JEALOUSY

And the spirit of jealousy come upon him, and he be jealous of his wife, and she be defiled; or if the spirit of jealousy come upon him, and he be jealous of his wife, and she be not defiled—Numbers 5:14.

- jealousy
- anger, wrath, rage
- murder
- revenge
- hate
- cruelty
- suspicion
- covetousness
- unnatural competition
- self-centeredness

- insecurity
- distrustfulness
- hard-heartedness
- feeling of being less loved by God than others
- builds walls in a person's life through hurt and anger, etc. (won't be vulnerable)
- divorce
- division
- abortion

13. SPIRIT OF STUPOR (OR SLUMBER)

According as it is written, God hath given them the spirit of stupor, eyes that they should not see, and ears that they should not hear: unto this very day—Romans 11:8.

- constant fatigue
- passivity
- "wallflower"
- procrastination
- self-pity

- blocks success
- draws back from life
- causes a person not to want to be born
- human spirit is asleep

14. Spirit of error

We are of God: he that knoweth God heareth us; he that is not of God heareth not us. Hereby know we the spirit of truth, and the spirit of error—1 John 4:6.

- irresponsibility
- immaturity
- inappropriate thinking
- inappropriate behavior
- confusion
- bulimia
- anorexia
- continuously making wrong decisions
- doubt

- unbelief
- deception
- compromise
- anti-Semitism
- intellectualism
- cults (false doctrines)
- false teachers
- false prophets and preachers
- false tongues
- racism

DEATH

Death is not called a spirit in Scripture, but it acts like a root spirit and it definitely can be a curse.

Forasmuch then as the children are partakers of flesh and blood, he also himself took part of the same; that through death he might destroy him that had the power of death, that is, the devil; and deliver them who through fear of death were all their lifetime subject to bondage—Hebrews 2:14–15.

People who have had near-fatal accidents, near-drowning experiences, death curses placed upon them (especially by their parents) those who have been nearly aborted, or have had repeated abortions have often been discovered to have death curses.

I had a death curse pronounced upon me from my birth. My father said, "I hope that little SOB never draws a breath; I hope he dies." I came from my mother's womb struggling for life. For the first year of my life, I battled to live.

Through the patient work of a family doctor who lived in the same house with my grandparents where I was born, I was nursed and cared for. Humanly speaking, by the hand of the doctor, I was kept alive for the first months of my life. Growing up, I had a number of near-death calls. Once again, I was spared from death by the hand of God.

When my son was born, throughout his early years of life, he had many close brushes with death. When he was about five or six years old, we moved into a new home which didn't have a fence around the yard. My son drove a riding-lawn mower off into a deep concrete drainage ditch that was about fourteen-feet deep and thirty-feet wide. He backed the mower into the ditch and rode it to the bottom! He could easily have killed himself.

In that same drainage ditch, when he was about seven years old, he had a stretched rope across it to swing on. When it rained, water came rushing down that drainage ditch. It would have been impossible for a child to survive if he had fallen into the water.

One day my son went out after it had rained. He got on the rope and began swinging back and forth. But he could not swing far enough to get back to the bank. He was hanging over the water, about to turn loose, when I walked out into the backyard with a friend and happened to notice the rope swinging. I ran over to him, pulled him up out of the drainage ditch. He said, "Dad, I was just about to turn loose because I couldn't hold on any longer." Again, a near-death experience.

Death curses come in many people's lives. We call them accidents, but they may have been pronounced upon us and handed down to us under the tutelage of the kingdom of darkness.

SHINING LIGHT ON THE SHADOWS

If these fourteen root systems are producing fruit of any kind in your life, you need to have these strongholds pulled down and the root systems cut out. This is what deliverance ministry is all about—shining the light of truth into the dark places deep within your spirit.

A deliverance session provides a time and place to openly renounce any unconfessed sin and the satanic lies you have long believed. Then you can slam shut doors you may have had open in your life. Only then can you walk free from the iniquities that have been handed down to you, through your ancestry, willful sin, unforgiveness, trauma, or an inner vow or judgment. Satan is very serious about bringing you into bondage and keeping you there. Jesus is very serious about getting you out.

The reason the Son of God appeared was to destroy the devil's work—1 John 3:8b.

Before approaching deliverance, spend some time thinking about your life. What issues have continually haunted you? In what ways have you disobeyed God's voice? What shadows do you continue to fight over and over? What part of the fight is yours, and what part was handed down to you from your parents or grandparents? What are the strongholds Satan has orchestrated in your life? Who have you not forgiven?

Now carefully walk through all of the fourteen root spirits and their fruit. Pray and ask the Holy Spirit to show you any strongholds or curses that are in operation in your own life or in your ancestral line. Be honest with yourself and don't let the enemy lie to you any longer. Constantly remind yourself that any lie will bind you, but the truth will set you free.

Don't be surprised if you find strongholds in all fourteen root spirits. I've found that it is rare for anyone to have strongholds operating in any less than twelve of the fourteen root spirits! Remember, you are considering your family bloodline and ancestors as well as your own strongholds.

In the next chapter, we will discuss how to break these strongholds and close the five doors that provide Satan with legal access to your life. Hang on. Freedom is right around the corner.

CHAPTER 9

THE DELIVERANCE: 1-2-3 THEY'RE OUT!

The following case is extreme, but important in understanding how Satan's kingdom functions—even in some of your own communities! It's not told to scare or upset you, but to show the reality of the spiritual battle and the importance of the church recognizing that we are in a war. If not, many of our children will be lost to the kingdom of darkness. Jesus has already won the war. Thankfully, we too, have His authority to enforce the victory of the cross. Susan's story is proof of that victory.

SUSAN'S STORY

When Susan came to me for ministry, she had spent many years in counseling and psychiatric hospitals, where she had been diagnosed as having Multiple Personality Disorder (MPD). She had great difficulties in relationships including her marriage, in caring for herself, and in keeping or functioning on a job.

Susan had twelve distinct, definably different personalities which would emerge according to what was going on in the environment around her. Counselors had helped her as best they could, but Susan was still tormented and unable to function in most areas of her life.

Sitting in my office, Susan began to share her tragic story. She was born the second child of a family with a long history of heavy occult involvement. Her parents were highly respected and upstanding members of a church in a town totally controlled by a well-established group of Satan worshippers. These Satanists included town officials, the legal community, and the educators. Susan's father was a professional man and her mother was a homemaker.

Susan's childhood environment was made up of people who were deeply entrenched in the occult. She thought this was normal. She was raised to follow in her parents' footsteps. She was destined to be a "satanic plant" in a church. Her father was a church leader and her mother was a Sunday school teacher. Usually, "satanic plants" are prepared to function in either childrens' ministries or music ministries. Always highly trained, these "satanic plants" will have great expertise in the particular skill required as well as extensive Bible knowledge. They "seem" to be the perfect person for the job.

Susan said her mother functioned and performed perfectly in every task she did. However, she never displayed any love, and so there was no real life in her. Her parents were involved in training Susan as well as the children from other families in their occult community to be "satanic plants" in local churches.

At the age of six, Susan was involved in her first human sacrifice. She was told, "It is your life or this baby's life." She was forced to drink the blood and eat human flesh. From that time on, Susan observed numerous occultic rituals and was made to participate in all kinds of animal and human sacrifices.

These occult rituals used perverted actions to dishonor the Lord's supper, Christ's crucifixion, and other sacred doctrines of the church. This was done to destroy her ability to believe in Jesus as Lord and Savior. Her mother's assignment was to teach children in the church in such a way that they would believe in a form of Jesus, but never in the true Jesus of the Bible. At a certain age all the children were led to give mental assent to Jesus as their Savior but with no real conviction, no repentance, and no regeneration. Therefore, they would grow up thinking they were saved, but they were only members of a church having never been born again.

When Susan was eleven, she was "married" to her father in an occult ceremony which was finalized in blood and various sexual rituals. As she continued to be programmed by the occult, her personality began to split off in order to cope with the horrible activities and sights to which she was exposed. The occult training system was divided into twelve parts—one for each hour of the clock. These twelve divisions were marked by certain colors for each division and had men and women assigned to each of them. The same occult practices are utilized worldwide and, therefore, are easily recognized by all occult teachers and leaders no matter what their nationality might be.

Often Susan was taken away from school during different times of the day to be trained in one of the twelve areas. Each training session would be sealed in some kind of perverted sexual activity. No teachers complained about such absences because the school superintendent was also in the occult, and was simply instructed to let the children go.

Using a sophisticated system of authority as well as drugs and mind control to alter her personality, the leaders totally programmed Susan by their teaching and their acts. Her mind became so confused that she did not know the truth from a lie. She was taken to the church in the middle of the night to be a part of satanic rituals on the altar. These rituals were performed by naked men and women to profane the altars of God.

In spite of all that happened to Susan, God had a destiny for her. When she was in the fifth grade, she was born again at a vacation Bible school. Her mother got very sick that day and was not able to go and teach as she normally would. In her place God sent a loving woman from another town who came in to help with vacation Bible school. She presented to Susan the real Jesus, and Susan received Him as her Lord and Savior. So, through all the satanic indoctrination, part of Susan's heart could not be captured.

In my office that day, we demolished the strongholds in the twelve areas of the occult. We called Susan's soul back from all the men and women who had profaned her and made perverted soul ties with her. We asked God to bring her personality back to her, to make her one, to heal her, and to make her whole. Only a power encounter with Jesus could heal Susan's broken, fragmented, and segmented soul and spirit. Praise God! Today Susan says she is no longer MPD (multiple personality disorder) and is learning to lead a normal, fulfilling life as a fruitful member of a solid, Christ-filled church. She has broken all ties with her family and the curses associated with her ancestral heritage of divination and whoredom. The doors are closed, and she is free. To God be the glory!

Breaking a curse, casting out demonic spirits, or pulling down a stronghold is not something mysterious; it is a supernatural act of God that cannot be accomplished by man alone. A person who is under a curse or who has demonic strongholds in his or her life needs assistance from a qualified person with spiritual authority who knows how to war! A person in bondage cannot free themselves. If they could, he or she would have done it long ago.

The Formula

There is no set formula to follow in casting out demonic spirits and tearing down strongholds. You cannot put God in a box. It isn't the words of the person praying or the individual being prayed for, but rather the anointing that breaks the yoke. The power of God demolishes strongholds, and a power encounter with the God of truth is what you must have in order to break free in your life.

There is a plan to follow, but please do not attempt to do this alone. As mentioned in several of the examples found throughout the book, the spirits of darkness can manifest in many different ways. An experienced person of spiritual authority needs to be present with you as you pray for deliverance!

As you are led through each step, you may feel strange at times. Although no two sessions are alike, many people often report feeling dizzy, nauseous, disassociated, or nervous. Coughing, sneezing, choking, crying, heavy breathing, and even yawning are also common. Some people report feeling absolutely nothing at all, while others report experiencing gut-wrenching pain, often beginning as each root spirit is addressed and ending as it is told to leave.

Demons often cannot be seen by the person going through the deliverance. Or sometimes they appear as a wisp of smoke or a shadow as they depart. Whether or not the dark spirit is seen, when the demon has left, there is always a sense of release in the spirit of both the person who is praying and the one receiving deliverance. The dark place is gone and the Holy Spirit can now begin to fill it up!

I do not recommend, or see any reason to have, conversations with any of the spirits dealt with during deliverance. The purpose of a demon is to lie, deceive, and defile. Consequently, there is nothing to be accomplished by giving them a platform from which to speak.

Steps for Deliverance

Step 1: Are you a Christian? Have you confessed your faith in Jesus Christ and in the sacrifice that He has made on your behalf? It is absolutely necessary to know Christ before seeking deliverance, because without being able to walk in the Spirit and in the authority of Jesus, you won't remain free. You will end up in an even worse condition—seven times worse, than before the deliverance.

> *When an unclean spirit is gone out of a man, he walketh through dry places, seeking rest, and findeth none. Then he saith, I will return to my house from whence I came out; and when he is come, he findeth it empty, swept, and garnished. Then goeth he and taketh with himself seven other spirits more wicked than himself, and they enter in and dwell there; and the last state of that man is worse than the first. Even so shall it be also with this wicked generation—Matthew 12:43-45.*

> *The Spirit itself beareth witness with our spirit, that we are the children of God—Romans 8:16.*

At this point you cannot wonder if you are a child of God, or hope you are a child of God, you must know you have been bought with His blood and that you belong to Him.

Know who you are in Christ.

Step 2: Yield yourself completely to God, and depend totally on Him and His power to free you. God said that without Him you can do nothing. Without a complete surrender of your life to the will of God and without total dependence upon Him, knowing that you are not able to do anything but receive and appropriate what is already yours by the power of the Cross, you will not receive your deliverance. You may have some goose bumps running up and down your back. You may feel wonderful. But you will not be free from the strongholds of the enemy, unless God's anointing sets you free!

Step 3: Take away Satan's legal ground by closing any open doors.

DOOR OF ANCESTRAL AND OTHER CURSES

Jesus came to set you free from all ancestral curses as well as any other curses. He has given you the weapons of war that are needed to accomplish this.

Referring to the previous lists, identify any ancestral curses or other curses that need to be broken in your life. Ancestral curses originate in previous generations, but your own sins may have compounded their strongholds. Identify, confess, and repent of the specific sins and rebellion which led to developing the curses and strongholds in your life. You must realize how your actions have grieved God and then decide to stop repeating your sins.

Your sin may have also given cause for a curse to take root in your own generation. It must be broken to prevent it from being passed to future generations. Identify with the sins of your forefathers and confess that they have sinned. You are not trying to receive forgiveness on behalf of your forefathers; you are just confessing that, like you, your forefathers were sinners. This confession and identification is the first step in breaking the power of ancestral curses in your life.

True repentance means you agree with God.

If we confess our sins, he is faithful and just to forgive us our sins, and to cleanse us from all unrighteousness—1 John 1:9.

If you are unsure how to confess your sin, follow the following example of a prayer of forgiveness.

FORGIVENESS PRAYER

"Heavenly Father, I confess to You that I have sinned. (Name any specific sins that come to your mind.) Please forgive me of all my sin and rebellion against You. Cleanse me from all unrighteousness. I confess the sins of my ancestors and acknowledge that they were committed against You. I ask forgiveness for my sins and my ancestors' sins. Please forgive me for my part and my ancestors' part in (name any of the fourteen roots spirits that apply to you and your ancestors). Thank you, Lord, that I am forgiven by the blood of Jesus and the power of the Cross, according to Your Word. Amen."

After you have made a confession of your sins and asked God for forgiveness, make a confession of truth as to who you are in Jesus. Read aloud this prayer before the Lord:

CONFESSION OF TRUTH

"Heavenly Father, thank you that I have been bought and paid for by the blood of Jesus Christ. Since I have been bought and paid for, I am an heir of God and a joint-heir with Jesus. As a joint-heir, I live in Jesus and He lives in me. Since He lives in me, I have the right to overcome because He overcame. Now as an overcomer, I break every evil word, curse, and spell that has ever been spoken upon me. I take those words and nail them to the Cross and appropriate the power of the Cross in breaking every word ever spoken against me. Thank you that because of the exchange that took place at the Cross, I can receive Your mercy. I cancel any curse that has come, or would try to come, upon me through the sins of my forefathers to the third and fourth generations past. I take those curses and nail them to the Cross and appropriate the power of the Cross in breaking every curse.

"Your Word says that Jesus was made a curse for me. As a matter of fact, I place Jesus' Cross between me and the curses that would come upon me, so that when they come to me, they have to pass through the blood of the Cross. The blood of the Cross will transform them from a curse to a blessing. With an act of my will, I choose to receive every blessing that You, Heavenly Father, have for me.

"Now I take back any ground that I have ever given to any demonic spirit, whether knowingly or unknowingly. I renounce all contact with anything occultic or satanic. No evil spirit has any right or access to me. I cancel their lease on my life. I serve them their eviction notice. I declare them defeated in every area of my life.

"I specifically take authority over every evil spirit of infirmity, whoredom, bondage, perverseness, deaf and dumbness, lying, error, fear, divination, haughtiness, Antichrist, heaviness, jealousy, and slumber. I cut your chains. I break your bands. In the name of Jesus Christ I bind you and cast you out now. You have no place or memorial in me. You are defeated and cast down. I pull down every stronghold by the mighty name and authority of Jesus Christ, by His resurrection power, and by the power of the Cross.

Satan, you and all your demons are defeated and your power broken this day in my life. The old me died with Christ on the Cross; therefore everything from the kingdom of darkness has lost its hold on me, for I am a new creation in Christ Jesus. Amen."

RENOUNCING EACH SPIRIT

Go through each of the fourteen root spirits and, one-by-one, renounce any areas of fruit and strongholds in your life. For example, if you need to renounce the spirit of fear, cut its root, pull down its strongholds of inferiority, inadequacy, rejection, and so on. Break each fruit individually, and come against fear using spiritual warfare, until you sense a release in your spirit that the spirit of fear is gone and that its strongholds have been broken down. Renounce and break those curses pronounced upon you coming through from each one of these root spirits.

Next, turn to any other specific curses such as one spoken against you by a witch, someone in authority over you, words you yourself have spoken, or any ungodly oath you have taken. State what the curse involves, then pray this prayer:

BREAKING A WORD, OATH, OR CURSE

Father, I confess that I have sinned and have opened myself to Satan. I have received the curse of (name the curse). Forgive me for submitting and bowing down to the kingdom of darkness. I turn from Satan and this curse to You. Thank you, Lord Jesus, for breaking the curse. I now declare that these curses are broken in Jesus' name, Amen.

DOOR OF DISOBEDIENCE

Next, close the door of disobedience. You must be willing to accept full responsibility for your disobedience. You may have refused to do what God has said to do, or you may have done something He has said not to do.

Do not rationalize, justify, or try to blame others for your disobedience. Do not do as Adam did in the garden when he said, "Lord, it was this woman You gave me." Do not follow the example of Eve when she said, "Lord, it was the snake."

Acknowledge to God that you alone are responsible for your disobedience. Scripture says, "So then every one of us shall give account of himself to God" (Romans 14:12). Confess your sin, turn from it, repent of it, and thank God for cleansing you. Pray from a sincere heart, and be willing to accept God's forgiveness. Following is a sample prayer of repentance:

REPENTANCE PRAYER

Father, I confess that I have willfully chosen to rebel against You and disobey Your Word. Please forgive me. I now make the decision to turn from the sin of (name the sin or sins). I receive forgiveness through the blood and the name of the Lord Jesus Christ. Amen.

DOOR OF UNFORGIVENESS

To close the door of unforgiveness, you must forgive from your heart or spirit all those who have hurt, defrauded, or wronged you. Scripture says:

And when ye stand praying, forgive if ye have ought against any: that your Father also which is in heaven may forgive you your trespasses—Mark 11:25.

If someone has hurt you in times past and you have not truly and totally released and forgiven them from your heart, you need to offer a prayer of forgiveness for each person and release each one in your spirit. Following is a sample prayer:

Prayer for Forgiving Others

"Heavenly Father, I forgive (call person's name) from my heart for all the things he/she has done to me. (Tell God all they have done to you.) I let them go free. I lay nothing to their charge. I require nothing of them. I release them into Your hands, Father, for You to get vengeance as you so choose. I forgive (call name) from my heart for all the things he/she has done to me because You, Father, have already forgiven me, and I bless him/her in Jesus' name."

Now take the $12.50 notes you have with their name on them and tear them up completely and throw them away. Go to that room in your heart where you keep all the pain and emotional stuff against them. Now sweep that room clean. Keep back nothing. Let it all go. When you have swept it clean, close the door, and pray a blessing on them from God.

Not only should you forgive others; you must also forgive yourself. If you were involved in the kingdom of darkness, or bowed down to the will of the enemy and disobeyed the Lord, you must take yourself through this prayer. Forgive yourself for all the hurtful things you have done to yourself, confessing those things to God.

All past failures and events that have hurt and harmed you must be dealt with and left in the past. If you need to forgive someone, then you need to do that now. If you need to forgive God for letting a painful circumstance come about in your life, then you need to do that now. If you need to go and seek forgiveness from someone, then do it now. If you need to forgive yourself for the things you have done to yourself, do that now. Let cleansing take place in your life.

PRAYER FOR FORGIVING MYSELF

"Heavenly Father, I forgive myself for all the things I have done to myself. (Tell God what you have done to yourself.) I let myself go free. I lay nothing to my charge. I require nothing of myself. I release myself into Your hands, Father, to get vengeance as You so choose. I forgive myself from my heart for all the things I have done, because You, Father, have already forgiven me."

Now take the $12.50 notes with your name on them and tear them up completely. Throw them away. Now go to that room in your heart where you keep the memory and pain of all these events and sweep it all out and clean that room of junk you have kept there against yourself. Release it all!

DOOR OF INNER VOWS AND JUDGMENTS

To close this door, confess and renounce any inner vows you have spoken. You must know what the vow is before you can break it. You cannot say, "I break all the vows that I may have ever made." A vow isn't broken until you specifically name the vow on an individual basis.

Since vows are based on judgments which you have made against another person, pray and ask the Holy Spirit to bring to your mind any vow you have ever spoken against anyone. Write them down and then pray the following prayer. As you go through each vow, be specific. If you made several different vows against the same person, break each vow individually.

PRAYER FOR BREAKING A VOW

"Heavenly Father, I confess that my judgment of (name the person) was sin. I now repent from the judgment and from the making of this vow. I renounce this vow. In Jesus' name I break the vow of (specifically repeat the vow that was spoken). I speak to my spirit and withdraw the words spoken. I call back the assignment in the heavenlies and cancel the words. I cast the words at my feet and break their power over my spirit, my thoughts, my emotions, my decisions, and my body. Any demons assigned to carry out this vow are now reassigned to dry places. I declare that this vow has no effect upon me—body, soul or spirit. Thank You, Lord Jesus, for breaking this vow and restoring my relationship with You and with (name the person you judged). Praise You, Lord, that as I pray right now I am free from this vow. Amen."

DOOR OF EMOTIONAL HURTS AND TRAUMA

To close the door of emotional hurts and traumas, begin by reading this passage from Isaiah:

Surely, he hath borne our griefs, and carried our sorrows: yet we did esteem him stricken, smitten of God, and afflicted. But he was wounded for our transgressions, he was bruised for our iniquities: the chastisement of our peace was upon him; and with his stripes we are healed. All we like sheep have gone astray; we have turned every one to his own way; and the Lord hath laid on Him the iniquity of us all—Isaiah 53:4-6.

Ask the Holy Spirit to come and heal the wounds and bruises in your emotions and spirit. These wounds are not just in your mind; they

have impacted your entire life. Bruising is caused by an internal hemor-
rhaging, and your spirit has been bruised by the enemy. Severe rejection,
hurtful words that people have said to you, near-death experiences,
deaths of family members, and divorce cause trauma and emotional
pain that need to be healed. Open your heart and let Jesus heal you.

To have a divine encounter with God's power, you will need to
cooperate with His Spirit. The Holy Spirit will come upon you, but
you must allow the pain of the trauma to come up. Release the pain,
give it up to Him, and let Him heal your emotions. Only upon releasing your pain to the Lord will you be healed.

PRAYER FOR EMOTIONAL HEALING

Lay your hands upon your chest and open your heart to God. Pray this
prayer: "Heavenly Father, I ask that you come now and take the pain,
hurts, and trauma from my spirit. I give you my pain and hurt. Take
my pain, Lord Jesus. Take the pain of (name specific hurts). Heal my
heart and set me free. Take my pain now."

Keep repeating the prayer noting specific hurts and pains until you
go through all the trauma in your life, asking Jesus to heal and remove
the pain.

Step 4: Pray for a fresh infilling of the Holy Spirit. We are to be
filled with the Holy Spirit (Ephesians 5:18). Ask God to fill all the
places vacated by the kingdom of darkness with the fullness of
Himself. Wait for God's Spirit to come upon you and fill you with His
presence. Often, you will experience a peaceful resting of the Spirit of
God upon you. Yield and wait for Him.

Step 5: Realize that you are dead to sin. By faith, reckon yourself dead to your sinful urges and desires (Romans 6:1-14). By faith, believe that you have received God's blessings. Even if you may have done some terrible things, the blood of Jesus forgives them all. If you have confessed your sins, then turn from them and walk each day toward all God has in store for you!

Step 6: Give praise and glory to God for your deliverance from the bondage of the enemy. Praise the Lord for His wonderful deliverance in your life: freedom from curses, freedom from the sin of disobedience, freedom from the torments of unforgiveness, freedom from the pain of emotional trauma, and freedom from being stuck on a path of defeat and failure by the vows you had made. Give God praise for His mighty, wonderful works!

PSALM 34

I will bless the Lord at all times; his praise shall continually be in my mouth. My soul shall make her boast in the Lord: the humble shall hear thereof, and be glad. O, magnify the Lord with me, and let us exalt his name together. I sought the Lord, and he heard me, and delivered me from all my fears. They looked unto him and were lightened: and their faces were not ashamed. This poor man cried, and the Lord heard him, and saved him out of all of his troubles. The angel of the Lord encampeth around about them that fear Him, and delivereth them. O, taste and see that the Lord is good: blessed is the man that trusteth in Him. O, fear the Lord, ye his saints: for there is no want to them that fear him. The young lions do lack and suffer hunger: but they that seek the Lord shall not want any good thing. Come, ye children, hearken unto me: I will teach you the fear of the Lord. What man is he that desireth life, and loveth many days, that he may see good? Keep thy tongue from evil, and thy lips from speaking guile. Depart from evil, and do good; seek peace, and pursue it. The eyes of the Lord are upon the righteous, and his ears are open unto their cry. The face of the Lord is against them that do evil, to cut off the remembrance of them from the earth. The righteous cry, and the Lord heareth, and delivereth them out of all their troubles. The Lord is nigh unto them that are of a broken heart; and saveth such as be of a contrite spirit. Many are the afflictions of the righteous: but the Lord delivereth him out of them all. He keepeth all his bones; not one of them is broken. Evil shall slay the wicked: and they that hate the righteous shall be desolate. The Lord redeemeth the soul of his servants: and none of them that trust in him shall be desolate.

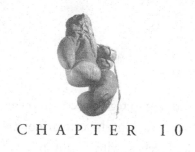

HANGING UP THE GLOVES

When you are called by God to become a champion of His Light, there is no hanging up the gloves! As you begin to dismantle personal strongholds and experience inner healing from emotional wounds, you will begin your life of freedom. Once God sets you free, you must stand resolute in that freedom.

> *Stand fast therefore in the liberty by which Christ has made us free, and do not be entangled again with a yoke of bondage....For you, brethren, have been called to liberty—Galatians 5:1, 13.*

Deliverance from demonic spirits and receiving inner healing is a giant step toward freedom, but you must maintain your freedom by continually walking in freedom. The liberation you have experienced will not automatically be there a year from now, or even a week from now. Satan does not give up easily. Instead, he will test and tempt you in numerous ways, trying to regain access into your life.

Once you receive freedom, be careful not to live unrighteously. Instead, seek God wholeheartedly. Establish a daily lifestyle of righteous living.

Believe it or not, you can walk in continuous freedom for the rest of your life, experiencing grace with each passing year. You are not expected to spend the rest of your life in a boxing match with the devil—trying to outrun him, outsmart him, or outdo him. God only asks you to resist the devil. If you follow these life principles, you will walk in freedom for the rest of your life.

Step 1: The Holy Spirit will empower you to live a godly life. Ask to be filled with His presence daily. Submit to the Holy Spirit. Know that He is constantly with you.

If you merely try to discipline your flesh or focus on following a list of do's and don'ts to accomplish the will of God, you will be living under law. Living legalistically will only make the desire to sin stronger in your life. God gives us the power to walk in freedom, not to walk in rules and regulations that make us look good. Don't try to act religious. Just be who you are—His precious child.

> *Therefore do not be unwise, but understanding what the will of the Lord is. And do not be drunk with wine, which is dissipation; but be filled with the Spirit—Ephesians 5:17–18.*

Step 2: Each morning yield yourself to God. Ask Him to take control of your life and guide you. Scripture says:

> *Trust in the Lord with all your heart, and lean not on your own understanding; in all your ways acknowledge Him, and He shall direct your paths—Proverbs 3:5-6.*

God directs your life by speaking to your spirit through the Bible, the Holy Spirit, and various life situations. He will direct you, but you must yield yourself to Him daily.

Step 3: As the Holy Spirit leads, make restitution to anyone you have wronged. God will bring individuals to mind and show you how to make amends for the wrongs committed.

Therefore if you bring your gift to the altar, and there remember that your brother has something against you, leave your gift there before the altar, and go your way. First be reconciled to your brother, and then come and offer your gift. Agree with your adversary quickly while you are on the way with him, lest your adversary deliver you to the judge, and the judge hand you over to the officer, and you are thrown into prison—Matthew 5:23-26.

If you have an issue against another person, settle it and be reconciled. If you have mistreated someone, ask their forgiveness. Do whatever you need to do to restore the relationship with the person.

Step 4: Ask the Holy Spirit to show you anything that needs to be removed from your home. Take away anything that could be associated with the kingdom of darkness—a figurine, an object, a book. Be sure to not destroy another person's property without their permission!

JAN'S STORY

A few years ago, Jan witnessed a strange, demonic phenomenon in her home. When she would go to bed at night, she sensed "something" walking around on her bed. Working at a high school, Jan was counseling gang members and trying to keep these troubled kids in school. However, she did not realize that some of them were Satan worshippers.

About fifteen of them had given her pictures they had drawn of demonic faces. Jan had put these in a file and brought them home. Apparently the teenagers had assigned curses to these drawings. These fifteen sheets of paper gave demonic spirits the right to come into Jan's home and torment her.

As we searched her home, the Holy Spirit showed us these fifteen sheets of paper with demonic faces drawn on them. Being led by the Holy Spirit, we burned the drawings in her fireplace which took away the legal ground the enemy had to enter her home. By faith, we also severed any demonic assignments placed on her life. Ever since, Jan has been free of demonic harassment in her home.

Step 5: Establish a new mind-set and identify yourself with the purposes and the plans of God. Truth is what God's Word says about you, not what someone else says or what you have believed about yourself. Continually remind yourself of God's truth. Read the following declaration of faith aloud several times each day. Wash your mind with His Word:

That He might sanctify and cleanse her by the washing of water by the word—Ephesians 5:26.

Consider offering this declaration as a prayer to God:

DECLARATION OF FAITH

"Heavenly Father, I choose to believe what Your Word says about me (Isaiah 40:8) rather than my carnal thoughts and feelings (2 Corinthians 10:4). My unbelief has been sin (Romans 14:23).

"Thank you, Lord Jesus, for loving me and dying on the Cross for my sins (Romans 5:8). Thank you that now there is no condemnation because I am in You (Romans 8:1). All of my past, present, and future sins have been forgiven (Ephesians 1:7) and cleansed by Your blood (1 John 1:7). You demonstrate perfect love toward me (1 John 4:18); therefore, I have nothing to fear. Thank you that nothing can touch me unless it is filtered through You and that all things work for my good and Your glory (Romans 8:28). Your love for me is unconditional (John 15:9) and everlasting (Jeremiah 31:3). I open my heart and life to Your love. Please flow Your love through me (Romans 5:5).

"Jesus, You know everything about me (Psalm 139:1-4) and yet You accept me just as I am (Ephesians 1:6). You made me unique and special to fulfill Your plan (Ephesians 2:10). Thank you for my body, my abilities, my parents which You designed as a part of Your perfect plan (Psalm 139:14). Thank you for the Holy Spirit who lives within me to empower me to obey You (Ephesians 3:20). Thank you that I am complete in You (Colossians 2:10).

"You have given me all spiritual blessings in Christ Jesus (Ephesians 1:3). Your strength is adequate for every task; Your grace is sufficient for every trial (2 Corinthians 12:9). I can do all things through You, Lord Jesus (Philippians 4:13). Thank you that You will perfect Your plan for me (1 Thessalonians 5:23-24). You are faithful even when I am not (2 Timothy 2:13). You promised never to leave me (Hebrews 13:5). Even now, You are changing me into Your image (2 Corinthians 3:18). I will not be foolish by comparing myself with others (2 Corinthians 10:12, 5).

"Father, how good it is to be Your child and to belong to You (1 John 3:1). That makes me Your responsibility (John 15:16), so I give myself completely to You. Whatever is accomplished in and through my life, You will have to do it (John 15:5; Philippians 2:13). Thank you for the confidence that You will! (Philippians 1:6). Praise be to You!"

The following statements summarize your scriptural identity and position in Christ. They form the foundation for your newfound freedom. Read these statements aloud often. If you are presently involved in a spiritual conflict, read these statements aloud, at least once a day for one month. Get them into your spirit. Meditate on them. God's truth will set you free!

Each day, take one of these truths and repeat it aloud, personalizing it. Meditate on it throughout the day.

THE LIE	THE TRUTH
I am rejected.	*I am accepted. (Ephesians 1:6; Psalm 139:17)*
I feel guilty.	*I am totally forgiven. (Ephesians 1:7; Psalm 103:3; Hebrews 10:17)*
I feel inadequate.	*I am adequate. (Philippians 1:7; 2 Corinthians 3:5)*
I am a fearful, anxious person.	*I am free from fear. (2 Timothy 1:7; 1 John 4:18)*
I am not very smart.	*I have God's wisdom. (1 Corinthians 1:30; Colossians 2:3)*
I am in bondage.	*I am free. (2 Corinthians 3:17; John 8:36)*
I am unlovable/ unloved.	*I am very loved. (John 15:9; Ephesians 2:4-5)*
I am unwanted.	*I have been adopted by God and am His child. (1 John 3:1; Romans 8:16-17).*
I am hopeless.	*I have all the hope I need. (Romans 15:13; Psalm 31:24)*

I have no strength.	*I have God's power. (Ephesians 1:1; Ephesians 3:20)*
I feel condemned.	*I am blameless. (Romans 8:1; John 3:18)*
I am alone/feel alone.	*I am never alone. (Hebrews 13:5-6; Romans 8:38-39)*
I have no one to take care of me.	*I am protected/safe. (Psalm 32:7-8; 10-11)*
There is nothing special about me.	*I have been chosen by God. (1 Corinthians 6:11; 1 Peter 2:9-10)*
I am not good enough.	*I am perfected in Christ. (Hebrews 10:14; Colossians 2:9-10)*
I am defeated.	*I am victorious. (2 Corinthians 2:14; Romans 8:37)*
I am afraid of Satan.	*I have authority over Satan. (Luke 10:19; 1 John 4:4; 1 John 3:8)*
I can't reach God.	*I have access to God. (Hebrews 10:19-22; Ephesians 3:12)*
I feel inferior.	*I am designed uniquely for God's purposes. (Psalm 139:13-14; Romans 2:11)*

Establish a new mind-set by memorizing the Word and thinking God's thoughts. Scripture says:

And do not be conformed to this world, but be transformed by the renewing of your mind, that you may prove what is that good and perfect will of God—Romans 12:2.

Not being "conformed to this world" simply means not being pushed into the world's mold, but being made new day-by-day by renewing of your mind, memorizing Scripture, believing it, and acting upon it. Establish this new mind-set by being confident in the truth that God loves you, that your sins are forgiven, and that you have been given the righteousness of God in Christ.

Step 6: To walk in freedom, you must stop talking and fellowshipping with demons! You may think you are just thinking about a certain event or some past action, when the enemy is really getting you to replay your past "videos." Refuse to replay the videos of past failures, hurts, sins, problems and difficulties, and who did you wrong. You have become a new person:

> *Therefore, if anyone is in Christ he is a new creation; old things have passed away; behold, all things have become new—* *2 Corinthians 5:17.*

When you became a believer, your old self died with Christ. Your sins were buried with Him, including your past. As far as God is concerned, that's all over. God does not want us to fellowship with demons. He wants us to fellowship with Him.

You may be wondering, "How do I take control of my mind when evil thoughts begin to come? Go to God's Word:

> *For the weapons of our warfare are not carnal but mighty in God for pulling down strongholds, casting down arguments and every high thing that exalts itself against the knowledge of God, bringing every thought into captivity to the obedience of Christ, and being ready to punish all disobedience when your obedience is fulfilled—2 Corinthians 10:4–6.*

Recognize which thoughts are not from God and rebuke those thoughts. Order the enemy to leave you "in the name of Jesus." Meditate on the Word of God and praise the Lord out loud for His blessings. Learn to live a life of constant thanksgiving and praise to God.

You are given the name of Jesus and the blood of Jesus as a mighty weapon. Whenever the enemy comes against you, plead the blood of Jesus. Declare that you have power in the mighty name of Jesus. Use the Word of God as a mighty instrument of war. Use your shield of faith to resist all of the fiery darts of the enemy. Use the spiritual armor God has given you.

Remember, putting on the armor of God is not a mystical thing. When you get up in the morning, mentally dress yourself. Speak aloud that you are placing on the breastplate of righteousness (the righteousness of Jesus). Put on the helmet of salvation so Satan's fiery darts cannot torment your mind. Put on the shoes that bring the gospel of peace. Place around you the belt of truth. You are not just saying words. You are claiming and appropriating what those pieces of armor are designed to do for you.

Use the word of your own testimony. Scripture says, "And they overcame him (Satan) by the blood of the Lamb and by the word of their testimony" (Revelation 12:11). Declare that you have been bought by the blood of Jesus. Declare that you are more than an overcomer because you are in Christ Jesus and Christ Jesus is in you. Declare that because He overcame, you have the right to overcome. Praise God for His many blessings toward you. Demons hate praise. Use the power of the Cross.

Ask God to surround you with His angels. Scripture says that angels are "ministering spirits sent forth to minister for those who inherit salvation" (Hebrews 1:14). Throughout the Old and New

Testaments are examples of how angels ministered to people like Paul and to our Lord Jesus when He was in the wilderness being tempted. Angels still minister to the saints of God today.

For He shall give His angels charge over you, to keep you in all your ways. In their hands they shall bear you up, lest you dash your foot against a stone—Psalm 91:11-12.

Step 7: God is calling you to a life of righteousness. So, treat all sin as if it were a rattlesnake! You wouldn't crawl in bed with a rattlesnake, even if it was just a little rattlesnake. Treat all sin in your life as if it were a biting viper—it is! You cannot make compromises for the flesh and give any place to the devil. Bring your flesh under the control of God. Scripture says to "put on the Lord Jesus Christ and make no provisions for the flesh, to fulfill its lust" (Romans 13:14).

Step 8: When you fail or sin, immediately confess it. Be cleansed, refilled, and continue to walk with Jesus. In our humanness, all of us will fall or fail from time to time. You do not have to punish yourself or hide from God. Jesus' death at the Cross has already paid for all of your sins. You were already forgiven before your sin was ever committed.

There is therefore now no condemnation to those who are in Christ Jesus, who do not walk according to the flesh, but according to the Spirit—Romans 8:1.

Step 9: There is no such thing as an empty mind. If you are busy doing the right things, you will not have as many temptations to do sinful things. Immediately replace negative activity and thinking with the positive. Fill your life with good things—helping others, encouraging others, giving to others and whatever the Holy Spirit prompts you to do. Scripture says that when we walk in the Spirit, we will not fulfill the lust of our flesh (Galatians 5:16). This means the Holy Spirit's power will enable me to walk in God's ways and to empower me to not fulfill fleshly lusts that war against me.

> *Rejoice in the Lord always. Again I will say, rejoice! Let your gentleness be known to all men. The Lord is at hand. Be anxious for nothing, but in everything by prayer and supplication with thanksgiving, let your requests be made known to God, and the peace of God which surpasseth all understanding will guard your heart and mind through Christ Jesus. Finally, brethren, whatever things are true, whatever things are noble, whatever things are just, whatever things are pure, whatever things are lovely, whatever things are of good report, if there is any virtue, and if there is anything praiseworthy—meditate on these things—Philippians 4:4–8.*

Step 10: Cultivate fellowship with other believers. Find a Bible-believing, Jesus-loving, God-fearing, Spirit-filled church. Make friends with other believers who want to know God deeply. Learn and grow together. Take yourself away from relationships with people who are walking in directions that lead you away from God and entice you to sin. Remember, "Do not be deceived: evil company corrupts good habits" (1 Corinthians 15:33).

Although it's natural to want to share Christ and be a testimony to your old friends, you must first learn to walk in freedom. Multitudes of believers have been pulled back into sin by this sly ploy of the enemy. Don't be deceived into thinking it can't happen to you!

Establish godly habits. Get into the Word, pray, and walk in the Spirit each day. Ask the Lord to show you how to change your routines. Don't give up, no matter how many times you fall. Persevere. Get back up, repent, and start again. You cannot change your routines simply in the flesh, but you can in the Spirit. Whatever it takes to establish and maintain new habits of righteousness, do it!

Step 11: Focus on getting to know God better and better. What is He really like? Learn to hear God's voice. He is always speaking, you just have not always been listening to Him!

God is continually giving us instructions, but usually we do not pause long enough to listen. No wonder the Lord says, "Be still, and know that I am God" (Psalm 46:10). If we are constantly rushing about or talking, we cannot hear His still small voice.

Sit quietly before the Lord. Listen to Him. Read His Word. Seek to know His ways. As you fellowship and make friends with God, you will begin to know Him—His attributes, His heart, and His ways.

Step 12: God wants instant obedience so learn to instantly obey Him. When the Holy Spirit prompts you to do something, don't argue or try to justify why you can't do it. Remember that as you obey God, He will reveal more of Himself to you.

God is serious about instant obedience. Doing something next month that God said for you to do last week is not obedience. Obedience is doing what you are told, when you are told, and how you are told to do it. God wants you to regularly hear His voice and spontaneously obey Him with a joyful heart. Take heart in the fact that the ways of the Lord are perfect and will lead you in perfect freedom. You can continue to walk in freedom because His truth always sets us free (John 8:32).

CONCLUSION

It is my prayer that you will experience the freedom that Jesus intends for you. Becoming liberated is an ongoing process that takes place throughout our lifetime.

Getting free is often like peeling an onion, it occurs one layer at a time. If you will apply the principles and truths in this book, you will experience freedom. Remember, you have been given all the authority you need to walk as a child of Light. The victory of the Cross is yours. Jesus has already won the war. Don't lose the battle. You will win if you don't quit!

Dr. Henry Malone, co-founder of Vision Life Ministries, had been a senior pastor for 28 years. Since 1989, he has ministered around the world with an emphasis on proclaiming and demonstrating the works of the Kingdom of God. A popular conference speaker and teacher, Henry also provides one-on-one deliverance ministry to those seeking greater freedom.

Since 1992, Henry has trained and released interns to serve in the local church. In 1998, he began the Personal Development Institute with the desire to help local churches establish effective deliverance ministries. Henry designed a four-stage training program to assist local churches. Each year, Henry also helps train pastors in several third-world nations and travels to churches and conferences speaking on behalf of world missions.

Henry and his wife Tina have two grown children, four grandchildren and live in Dallas, Texas area.

INDEX

TAKE BACK SPIRITUAL GROUND

by
Dr. Malone

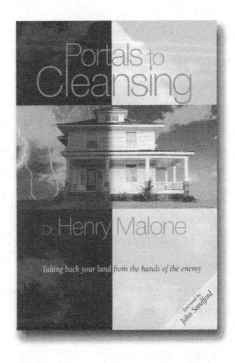

Portals—they exist all around the earth and open a door to the presence of God or to the demonic. Step into the realm of the supernatural with *Portals to Cleansing*. Discover how spiritual ground is taken and how it is released. Learn the keys to reclaiming your land, home, possessions and animals from the power of Satan and his demonic forces. Experience the peace that comes from the cleansing of all you possess. Walk into a portal of God's presence that will take you deeper into the realm of the Spirit and change your life forever.

Now Available

$10

Also available by Dr. Malone

FREEDOM AND FULLNESS SEMINAR

This 2-day seminar is an in-depth look at the 2-5-14 strategy. It is specifically designed to lead a church or group through corporate deliverance. Typically, the seminar begins on a Friday night and continues through late afternoon on Saturday with intensive teaching and ministry time. The seminar is led by a teaching team and a ministry team that have been trained or is the process of being trained by Vision Life Ministries.

PERSONAL MINISTRY TRAINING

The three-course Personal Ministry Training will encourage, train and equip those who desire wholeness in their own lives and desire to extend the Kingdom of God through deliverance and inner healing. Personal Ministry Training One develops the strategy of the warrior and focuses on training for leading a personal ministry session. Personal Ministry Training Two develops the heart of the warrior and focuses on the attitudes and character necessary to be fruitful and effective in ministry. Personal Ministry Training Three develops the gifts and skills of a warrior. It focuses on demonstration and participation in actual personal deliverance sessions. Each PMT is offered in a Thursday night, Friday and Saturday format. The Freedom and Fullness Seminar is a prerequisite to the Personal Ministry Training.

For churches or individuals who would like more information on these exciting and life-changing resources, please contact:

Vision Life Ministries
P.O. Box 292455
Lewisville, TX 75029
www.visionlife.org

ORDER FORM

■ Postal orders: **Vision Life Ministries, P.O. Box 292455, Lewisville, TX 75029**

■ Order online: **www.visionlife.org**

■ For more information, email: **info@visionlife.org**

Title	Price	Quantity	Amount
Islam Unmasked	$10	x_____	= _____
Portals to Cleansing	$13	x_____	= _____
Portals to Cleansing Kit	$13	x_____	= _____
Shadow Boxing	$13	x_____	= _____

Shipping and Handling_____
(Please add $6.50 for the first book and $2 for each additional book)

Total_____

_____Please send more information about Freedom and Fullness seminars

_____Please send more information about Personal Ministry Training

_____
Name (please print clearly)

_____
Address   Apt.

_____
City   State   Zip

_____
Country   Phone

_____
E-mail

Method of Payment

___Check/Money Order (payable to Vision Life Ministries)   ___Visa   ___MasterCard

_____
Card Number   Expiration Date

_____
Card Holder (please print clearly)

_____
Signature